THE VANISHING ADOLESCENT

The Vanishing Adolescent

By Edgar Z. Friedenberg

WITH AN INTRODUCTION BY DAVID RIESMAN

GREENWOOD PRESS, PUBLISHERS
WESTPORT, CONNECTICUT

Library of Congress Cataloging in Publication Data

Friedenberg, Edgar Zodiag, 1921-
   The vanishing adolescent.

   Reprint. Originally published: Boston : Beacon Press,
c1964.
   1. Adolescence. 2. Adolescent psychology. 3. Youth--
United States. I. Title.
HQ796.F77 1985   305.2'35   85-950
ISBN 0-313-24920-2

Reprinted with the permission of Beacon Press

Reprinted in 1985 by Greenwood Press
A division of Congressional Information Service, Inc.
88 Post Road West, Westport, Connecticut 06881

Printed in the United States of America

10 9 8 7 6 5 4 3 2 1

Acknowledgments

I am most grateful to my colleagues, Lenore Boehm, Bill and Nancy Connor, Al and Lu Gorvine, Brenda Lansdown, Mike and Jean Miller, Martin and Marilyn Nass, Carl and Jane Nordstrom, David Riesman, and Austin and Tess Wood, for their comments, criticisms, and sympathetic silences. The last three went to the trouble of preparing detailed and analytical criticism of an early draft, which proved indispensable to me.

In addition, I would like to thank the following publishers for permission to quote from their works:

Harcourt, Brace and Company
> For *The Cocktail Party* by T. S. Eliot and *Three Cheers for Democracy* by E. M. Forster

Harper & Brothers
> For *The Authoritarian Personality* by T. W. Adorno, *et al.*

The Macmillan Company
> For "The Pangolin" from *Collected Poems* by Marianne Moore

Thomas Nelson & Sons
> For "Changing Concepts of Homosexuality in Psychoanalysis" by Clara Thompson in *A Study of Interpersonal Relations* edited by Patrick Mullahy

New Yorker
> For "The Study of Something New in History" by Eugene Kinkead

W. W. Norton and Company
> For *Childhood and Society* by Erik H. Erikson

University of Chicago Press
> For *Self-Perception in the University: A Study of Successful and Unsuccessful Graduate Students* by Edgar Z. Friedenberg and Julius A. Roth

Contents

Preface to the 1964 Edition

It is now nearly seven years since I wrote *The Vanishing Adolescent*, and five since it was published. When Beacon asked me whether I wished to revise the book, I decided at once that I did not. *The Vanishing Adolescent* is not, and was never meant to be, a textbook. It is a record, as internally consistent as I could make it, of my feelings, beliefs, and insights about adolescence at a particular time; and that record should stand. The book, moreover, says what I should still like to say, possibly because it is an even more personal statement than I realized when I wrote it—and in this age people, for better or for worse, change more slowly than the world they live in.

Nevertheless, it would not, of course, be the same book if I were writing it today. If one does not become wiser in seven years time—fatter years than most for me—at least one becomes foolish in a somewhat different way. At the time that I wrote the book I did not even realize that I was committing an audacity. I thought that the books I read—the good ones anyway—had mostly been written by people who wanted to say something, sat down and said it, and then tried to get somebody to publish what they had written. I knew this was risky, but I thought the risk a matter of simple mathematical probability, there being more aspiring authors than demand for books. I didn't know that books were usually artifacts that spring from negotiations between authors and publishers before a line has even been written. And if I had, I doubt if I would have started; I was writing partly because I wanted a chance for more direct expression than teaching in a city college affords; and if I had realized that I was probably swapping a modest place in a formal power structure for an equally modest place in an informal one, it would not have seemed worth while. But I was saved by my own naiveté. Writing *The Vanishing Adolescent* was a clear case of the bumblebee not knowing it and flying anyway.

I also did not perceive what the book's most perceptive reviewer*

---

* Bennet M. Berger, reviewing James S. Coleman's *The Adolescent Society*, Paul Goodman's *Growing Up Absurd*, and *The Vanishing Adolescent* in a comparative essay: "Adolescence and Beyond," in *Social Problems* (Vol. 10, No. 4, 1963), pp. 394-408.

saw at once as its chief limitation, though I think also its greatest strength. *The Vanishing Adolescent* is, among other things, a love story; and whatever one may do with love stories it is generally unwise to edit them seven years later. I knew, of course, how I felt, and still feel, about adolescents. But I did not know how specialized and solipsistic my awareness of them had become. I do not myself believe that one can learn anything important about anything except by loving—or possibly hating—it: without strong feeling there is simply not enough empathy available to transcend the barrier between one's own existential state and any other. But this is only one kind of knowledge, and in the age of science not a kind that is held in much esteem; we call it subjective and dismiss it as useless for purposes of external manipulation and control.

The Vanishing Adolescent is, I hope, utterly valueless as a tool for handling "teen-agers"; in fact, it is designed to break off in the administrator's hand. This has, I am sure, made it disappointing to readers who had hoped to use it as a guide in solving the problems of youth, and who sometimes complain to me that I do not tell them what to do about the conditions I discuss. But adolescents are not a problem to me, and I cannot write about them as if they were. I regard them as I do love and death, which are not problems, though they leave problems in their wake. Adolescents both comfort and terrify me by their very nature and existence. I once described to an acquaintance what I had seen at a large track meet, especially during the time *between* events when an endless procession of tall, calm-looking boys in snug, glowing warm-up suits jog or lope around the track in pride and self-absorption, singly or in twos and threes, or lie in the infield resting for their event, aloof and immanent. When I paused, he wanted to know who had won. If I had told him that I had just heard the Budapest Quartet playing Mozart, I suppose he might have asked the same thing.

When I wrote *The Vanishing Adolescent*, I had known only those adolescents who had permitted me to become their friend through the previous twenty-five years since my own adolescence began. This is really not as biased a sample as one might expect considering the opportunities it presents for unconscious selection and self-selection. Most adults treat adolescents more like things than people, and anyone who does not and who has some affection and respect for them is likely to be accepted. I don't know that most youngsters like me, but my presence makes it easier for them to like themselves, and this is enough to keep the relationship going. So I had got fairly close to hundreds of young men and women; but the very fact that my relationships to them had all become personal meant that what I knew about them was very much colored by my own needs and point of view. Still, I did know what they must be in order to make me feel about them as I did, and that is the main pillar on which *The Vanishing Adolescent* rests.

Except for the place described in the chapter on "Five Exemplary Boys," I had hardly set foot in a high school. But here I did what Anthony Trollope did in writing about the Anglican Church bureaucracy, of which he had no firsthand knowledge but whose functioning he described with uncanny accuracy. He had for some years been a member of the British postal bureaucracy, and he extrapolated his experience upwards, presumably. I had taught for some years in a municipal college whose mode of organization, governing board, and source of support were similar to those of the high school, and which was subject to the same political and social pressures. Its staff, however, are better educated than most high school faculties, and it holds a respected position among colleges in general. I assumed then that the things that were wrong with high schools would be much the same as the things that were wrong with my college, but that they would be worse in high school; especially since I teach people who are, or plan to become, high school teachers, and had some idea of what their limitations were.

But as a result of the publication of *The Vanishing Adolescent*, I have gotten to know more adolescents in a wider variety of relationships. I have also gotten to know more about high schools and their life in high schools. I have just finished spending a year intensively interviewing students in nine secondary schools on the East Coast in a study of the influence of high school experience on student values and creativity; two years earlier, I had spent a year interviewing college students almost as intensively in a study of the reasons why those who were succeeding in science or engineering at a time when these subjects were being very much stressed in the society nevertheless often chose to change to other fields. I know more about adolescents than I did seven years ago, not because I know them any better, but because I have known them under the ordinary circumstance of their lives, especially in school. And I have certainly learned a great deal about schools.

If a publisher, planning a new edition of the *Divine Comedy,* were to ask Dante whether he wished to revise his earlier statement in the light of his extensive subsequent opportunity for direct, personal observation, Dante would, I believe, find it hard to decide. "Believe me," he might reply, "it's better you shouldn't ask!" My own feeling about Chapters 3 and 4 is that they stand up well enough in that the things they deal with really do turn out to be the important issues in school life that affect adolescent growth and development. But they are understated. I had no adequate idea of the detailed physical intrusiveness and vulgarity of the high school. I knew it was constrictive but I didn't know it was so presumptuous: the corridor-passes, the wrangling over smoking, the dress regulations, the ill-tempered, belligerent little men and enormous, aggrieved women detached from their teaching duties to scream at students in the corridors and the cafeteria for, quite literally, "getting out of line." It is the *details* that matter and these one cannot possibly imagine till one has seen them: the librarians who refuse to admit a student to the library unless he is wearing a belt; the youngsters crouched in the corridor like see-no-evil monkeys during compulsory Civil Defense drills; the blatting jocularity and pompous patriotism that comes over the public address system into every corner. I had also not grasped the fact that students have no refuge or surcease from it; being used to colleges and college schedules, it just didn't occur to me that high school students have no unscheduled time whatever during the school day and cannot even go to the library to study except during library period without a special pass; that they have no club room of their own or any place where they can get off and be themselves. The whole experience of secondary education, I came to realize, is set up in such a way as to insure that individual adolescents will become alienated from their own inner-life; they are given no opportunity to examine it, and are punished if they permit it to direct their actions. The high school is generally even more Orwellian than my vision of it had been; and, as with Orwell, it is the little things, the endless specifics, each petty in itself, that really make up the effect. Nineteen-*sixty*-four? We are certainly running well ahead of schedule.

I had also completely failed to grasp how impersonal the high school environment had become; and this, I think, is probably something new that was not, indeed, nearly as true seven years ago. It would be hard to duplicate the experience of my "five exemplary boys" today, and that is a good thing. But the reason is that by now high schools have become so much blander and more homogenized that the interpersonal relations seem seldom to be there to violate: Kurt and Peter are less likely to be aware of each other, and Thomas no longer has much power to humiliate people, since they do not really feel bound to one another in a common social system very strongly. Colleges are much better in this respect. Youngsters in the same college do tend to have more in common, and, I think, to develop stronger though fearfully mixed feelings about one another; anyone who deals at all intimately with college students must expect to get snarled up from time to time in dangling and exposed relationships between people he did not even know were friends or enemies. For just this reason, administrative compromises and constraints are really insulting to students, they do break up values that the youngsters are generating for themselves and diminish their pride and stature. In high school, there just isn't usually much human interaction there to begin with. What takes place between people takes place elsewhere and afterwards.

I now believe that this is the inevitable price of an open society if it uses its schools—and all open societies do—primarily to equalize social and economic opportunity among individuals from widely disparate social groups. The school cannot, under these conditions, nurture warmth, intimacy, or deeply felt commitments between individuals. People whose backgrounds are very different can, and of course do, come to mean very much to one another, and enrich one another's lives; but this happens only when they are working together on something that has significance and poignancy for them. It does not happen when they are blandly striving against each other for a favorable position in transit, or going through the forms of democratic ritual in order to assure a school district that it is a community, when it is really nothing but the residue of some thousands of inhabitants' poorly realized and conflicting ambitions.

Therefore, it seems to me that the tone of my comments about the schools is too harsh, even though the schools are even worse than

I thought. The whole society is worse than I thought; and it is bad for more fundamental reasons and reasons that are merely the obverse of its most highly prized values. The fact is that we are not a freedom-loving people; one would think that dignity and privacy meant nothing to us, except that our zeal in denying them to our neighbors suggests that we do at least fear them. Americans, of course, are heterogeneous, though much less so than our numbers and diversity of origin would lead anyone to expect. But by and large, we are a nation of empiricists, which sounds better than what it turns out to mean: a mixed lot of sly, manipulative, anxious people deeply threatened by the vicissitudes of an absurd, dangerous, and rather contemptible economic system that they dare not challenge for fear of what their dissent will do to their future chances. As individuals, of course, most of us are a lot better than that: genuinely decent, kind-hearted, public-spirited, and generous of impulse. But these qualities don't count for very much when the actions to which they might lead are certain to be killed in committee somewhere between conception and delivery. Tolerance and generosity among us have become what we call a posture; they are the greasy-kid-stuff with which we slick down the fundamental hard-headedness—or bone-headedness—of our policy decisions, private and public.

The reason this brings me to the verge of a tantrum, if not of despair, is that I am forced to admit, now that I have seen them in school, that our adolescents are not really all that different from the adults they will become. I have, as I said in *The Vanishing Adolescent,* known some rough knights in my time; but, as Berger points out, they were rather exceptional. That they can exist at all is, I believe, enough to establish the moral thesis of my book—and a society that reduces them to the status of youth on the make is not so much damnable as damned. But *The Vanishing Adolescent* pictures the young as engaged in a gallant, if hopeless struggle with the timidity and corruption of the adult world, usually in the person of school officials; and it would have been more accurate to picture American youth rather as already deeply implicated in the deeds and values of their culture. Mostly they go along with it and sincerely believe that in doing so they are putting down troublemakers and serving the best interests of their community. They accept, by and large, the society they live in; its rewards are the rewards they seek; its sanctions are the sanctions they fear. The school is a specialized instrument for dealing with the young, and therefore the place where their socialization is accelerated—but it is, on the whole, neither better nor worse than the rest of society and its students, fortunately for it, cannot really imagine that it might be different.

Our problem is not conformity. There may indeed be too little of that. If the world is a jungle, then obviously one must dress for dinner in it, if only out of respect for the memory of the neighbor who is to be served as the main course. The difficulty is that we have only norms to conform to, rather than standards. Heisenberg's uncertainty principle, which is a cornerstone of modern physics, tells us, in effect, that in order to know where anything is we must make observations on it that inevitably interfere with its trajectory; and it is only our trajectory that we worry about; we couldn't care less where, who, or what we are now. Basically, we do not even *want* a community; for people like us, motels are just about right. The high school is a kind of motel, though less well-appointed than it might be.

It is probably inevitable, therefore, that the struggle over school integration should have become polarized around the issue of equal access to the school conceived as public accommodation for transients. This leaves out some values that might, one would think, have been seen as equally, if not more, important: the dignity of Negroes, and the value to whites and Negroes alike of getting to know each other intimately and to form interpersonal commitments deep enough to allow them to share experiences that have been so crucially and tragically different. Not much is said about this; and I gather that school administrators who are trying to manage integrated systems devoutly hope that it won't happen or even occur to parents that it might.*

Instead, the case for integration is generally made on the bases

---

* Cf. A. V. Cicourel and John I. Kitzuse, *The Educational Decision Makers* (Indianapolis, The Bobbs-Merrill Company, Inc., 1963), p. 27. "The students coming into the high school are randomly assigned to the four divisions, with some noteworthy exceptions. . . . The second exception is the separation of Negro students and their equal distribution among the four divisions. Again, it is not clear why the randomizing device is not used. It appears that this administration has been concerned with an unknown amount of Negro-white dating. The subject is a touchy one around the high school and we were discouraged from asking questions about it."

of equality of opportunity, and of the need to utilize and recruit talent from all social groups instead of wasting the potential of discriminated-against members of society. These issues, of course, have nothing to do with race as such; they have assumed a racial form because past and continuing mistreatment and rejection of Negroes have forced most Negroes into poverty and excluded them from the mainstream of the culture, such as it is. Since nearly all the recent examples of integrity and devoted social purpose to be found among Americans have been afforded by Negroes, discrimination must at least have had a beneficial tendency to reduce the temptation of Negroes to become like Jules Feiffer characters, but a people can hardly expect salvation because their own misconduct has unintentionally resulted in the moral preservation of some of their victims.

It may nevertheless cost the society more than it knows to seek out mute, inglorious Miltons among the poor, and incorporate them into the middle-class way of life. On the whole, I prefer Charles II, and maybe even Charles I, to Milton. We are inclined toward extravagant tolerance of defects of craftsmanship among self-made men; we forget how grandiose Milton was in vision, and how mean in practice. A social system which systematically scours its lower ranges for talent, and shoves the duller or less aggressive members of its established society out of St. Grottlesex and Harvard to make way for them, is also denying itself the fruits of a long process of social maturation. Talent searches, moreover, can only be conducted on terms set by the searchers; it is they who say what constitutes talent, and adolescents come to their attention by sedulously cultivating the qualities they are looking for, rather than by looking within themselves and cultivating what they find there. The emphasis in our talent search is in combing, with objective tests, through the dark and shamefully neglected discards of our youth in the hope of finding there something bright and sharp that can be put to good use; and I am sure that that there is plenty to be found that would otherwise be wasted. But I have not noticed any deficiency among us of people who are bright and sharp, and willing to be put unquestioningly to rather dubious service for the sake of rather dubious opportunity.

What I have noticed—and far more frequently than I thought when I wrote *The Vanishing Adolescent*—is young people who, having no concept of fixed stars, have also no gift for navigation.

Nor—and this is their grace and their tragedy—will they stay on the beam; they are sensitive and rightly distrust from the depth of their hearts the jolly establishment that transmits it; no love—and well they know it—inspires these nocturnal emissions. They fly blind, by the seat of their jeans that the high school forbids them to wear, and slip in an instant from positions of apparent stability into grotesque and dangerous patterns that could not, in any case, get them anywhere. Adults cannot tell where they are with them; but, then, they seldom are with them. It is a terrifying journey, and at the destination there is no visibility.

I have never been on it; I have not the courage to go, and am too old to be welcome. What I know about it comes from having run, for just thirty years, the lunch-room at one of the places they can sometimes touch down. We are integrated, the food is good, and we cannot afford much fog. Since *The Vanishing Adolescent* was published I have been moved to find that they sometimes carry it with them. Not as a working chart; for that purpose, like most charts, it was obsolete before it was printed. What youngsters like most about it, I believe, is the quaintly fanciful depiction of terrain they are more familiar with, and the deadly accuracy of the portions of it that are simply endorsed: "Here be dragons!"

E.Z.F.

Introduction

Mr. Friedenberg writes that "understanding . . . is more sustaining than cheerfulness." This book, with its argument that adolescence, and the kind of selfhood it may in the best cases bring, is disappearing in our society, exhibits great understanding, much passion and compassion, a leavening of irony, and precious little cheerfulness. Of all the wide-ranging diagnoses of our time, it is one of the most profound because it is at once intensely imaginative and empirically grounded: grounded in the social-psychological studies of adolescent character, of schools and teachers, and of the author's own observations as a teacher and teacher of teachers. I do not mean by this that Mr. Friedenberg proves his case on the basis of the studies he has done: he is not making a survey of modal adolescents, and the kinds of things he is saying, based for the most part on inferences concerning unconscious processes, are not in the state of the art of social science today subject to easy verification. It follows from this that THE VANISHING ADOLESCENT makes demands on the reader, or at least on this reader: not because the author writes obscurely—he writes delightfully—but because what he has to say is often original, hence elliptical, and because he deals with themes which bring home to every parent, teacher, or other adult facing adolescents what is emotionally and morally involved in this confrontation.

For one thing Mr. Friedenberg shows how a bureaucratic and equalitarian society such as ours is aggressively hostile to male homosexuality (shown, for instance, in the attacks of the McCarthyites on the alleged homosexuals in the State Department and high government service generally), and how the resulting panic fear of homosexuality tends to make many adult males overreact to adolescent boys and young men, sometimes treating them as vicarious bearers of their own suppressed energies and aims, and almost always communicating to them their own anxiety and lack of clarity of role. Mr. Friedenberg suggests that even in an aristocratic society like that of the pre-Socratic Greeks or the Kaiser's army corps homosexuality cannot be taken lightly, as simply one of man's many relativistic ways; but he does contend, I think correctly, that the kind of subjectivity and self-centeredness inherent in the homo-erotic man is especially anathema to a peer-oriented culture which stresses objectivity, fairness, and achieved rather than ascribed qualities. Correspondingly, the intense subjectivity of many ado-lescents, along with their partly physiological and partly culturally-conditioned sexuality, makes them a highly salient screen for adults whose own buried subjectivity remains as an unconscious threat to their ambitions for status and security. Such adults unconsciously insist that teen-agers vicariously act out what they themselves ambiv-alently fear: this is one source of the centrality of the teen-ager today as the symbol at once of the under- and the over-privileged, lacking the material possessions and position of adulthood but romantically clinging to the youth, ardor, and aristocratic integrity and insouciance which the adult has lost or surrendered. Indeed, I agree with the author: in a society which has increasingly enfranchised women, the poor, even the Negro, the adolescent becomes the favorite rebel with-out a cause—causeless because society seemingly asks so little of him, merely that he "grow up," finish school, and get on the payroll.

I have greatly foreshortened a subtle web of discourse. But Mr. Friedenberg makes wholeheartedly clear that he is on the side of the vanishing adolescent and in opposition to all the officials (teach-ers, guidance people, cops) and all the unofficials (disk jockeys, editors) who confuse youth and fail to give them a clear and dis-ciplined way of facing themselves and the world. He sees adolescent growth as naturally benign, though at the same time and inevitably in conflict with society; this conception casts adults in the role of *agents provocateurs*—though seldom consciously so—for whatever goes awry with youth. Like the author, I am impressed with the exceptional fineness of temper and interpersonal sensibility of the best young people today. And perhaps it reveals my own defensive-ness as parent and teacher that I am both frightened and depressed by the *Lumpenproletariat* of morally and culturally impoverished young whose basic passivity makes heroic demands on those who must daily cope with them in or out of school. In my view (but not, I think, the author's) adults are victims as well as victimizers.

In fact, Mr. Friedenberg much prefers the minatory teacher of the British public school, against whom an adolescent can define himself, to the more malleable teacher of the American public school; if the author must choose, he thinks children cope more readily with brutality than manipulation. I am less sure about this: most sensitive young people today, who give Mr. Friedenberg and me our affirmative picture of youthful decency and competence, are not the products of a brutal environment, though they have by-passed the more subtle traumas of a manipulative one. As a result, they are more vulnerable than their predecessors, more likely to deploy their virtues privately than publicly, but are otherwise more interesting, various, and open than the perhaps more self-reliant British ex-schoolboy.

But these are marginal shadings; and with Mr. Friedenberg's main point, I am in full agreement—namely, that traditional adolescence *is* vanishing, swallowed up at the childhood end by the increasing precocity of the young, their turning of high school into an *ersatz* college or even suburb, their early if somewhat flat maturity as lovers, consumers, committeemen; and at the adult end by the prolongation of the period of training for the increasing numbers in graduate school, a cadre caricatured by the psychoanalyst-in-training who at 40 is still his supervisor's "boy," dependent on his approval for certification, self-esteem, and patronage. Anyone who doubts the knowledgeability of the contemporary American teen-ager might be startled to realize that Charley Brown, the London evacuee who is the hero of Joyce Cary's *Charley is my Darling*, is 15; to an American reader he seems more like 12. Speaking of the moral experimentalism of children, Cary writes in his preface:

. . . the imagination is always looking for significance; both in the physical and moral world, that is its job, to put together coherent wholes, a situation with meaning, a place where the child does not know, all the time, where he is.

Mr. Friedenberg would agree; and would add that the American teen-ager, able to anticipate adulthood, so to speak, on the installment plan, gives up too readily his search for significance, settling (while Charley Brown, still confused, still searches) for a pliable and adjusted blandness.

Or if not that, then often for delinquency, which can be one response of a lower-class boy to his unease in a middle-class school and to his humiliations at the hands of adults, who may seem tough or merely too intrusive. In the delinquent gang such a boy finds support for his shaken self-esteem, though at the cost of drying up his own potentialities for humane responsiveness as well as for the middle-class success that seems either beyond reach or too abject a surrender of a brittle virility.

The author, while fully aware that the high school is the parochial captive of all articulate pressure groups in the community, still cannot hide his anger and despair at the large share the school has in creating, or not preventing, "adjustment" in the majority and "delinquency" in the minority of adolescent boys. (About girls, the book has much less to say, though what is said shows understanding; for instance, the observation that girls are far less vain and less moody than boys.) Mr. Friedenberg notes that schoolteaching is the most accessible profession for the moderately mobile but not basically ambitious children of the upper working class and lower middle class (engineering takes no more time but usually more brains and drive). Most schoolteachers never have the chance to come into contact with a disciplined mind and an alert imagination: asked to transmit a cultural heritage as alien to them as to many of their lower-status charges, they do so with the anxious passivity of petty civil servants. Fearful of surveillance by the community and its representatives, they naturally prefer the orderly children who are no trouble and who, in Mr. Friedenberg's definition, are not suffering adolescence. And when they must face a teen-ager who does make trouble, the teachers' lack of any personal authority leads them to try, not to clarify for the student his world and his conflicts with it, but often to confuse and humiliate him further as a way of shaming him into line.

One new technique for this has sprung up almost without anyone noticing: it is the dossier, the personnel folder which increasingly contains information on adjustment as well as on academic standing and the more obvious breaches of discipline. The author states that high school students are already quite aware of the threat by a teacher or guidance official that "this will go on your record," and is furious that the school has allowed itself to become, not

only a sorting station for academic aptitude, but a monitor for conduct and personality as well; he feels that this contaminates whatever confidential relations might develop between students and
staff. I know what he is talking about, for I know how miserable
I feel whenever an FBI or Army Intelligence agent comes to talk
with me about a student on whom a security check is being made:
if I should tell the agent that my relations with students are confidential, I would only uphold a general principle at the expense of
a particular student (as well as miss a chance of possibly getting
across to the agent that, e.g., socialists are not Communists and, if
one wants to catch or oppose Communists, socialists are about the
best allies one could find). The only solution I have seen—other
than the sensible one of abolishing security checks as a greater evil
than even an occasional uncaught spy—is that proposed by some
professors at the University of California: namely, an institution-
wide rule restraining faculty members from giving out information,
so that a refusal by a particular professor would no longer prejudice
his former students. I hope that Mr. Friedenberg's protest may stir
the professional associations of schoolteachers and guidance people
to similar stratagems for preventing the abuse of their ability to
find out more about youngsters than previous generations of teachers
had time for, cared about, or knew about.

All this is made painfully vivid by Mr. Friedenberg's description of his visit to the student court at a public high school, a court
at which bland yet self-mistrustful "leaders" judged, badgered, and
shamed boys who had broken school rules. Through interviews and
projective tests (the latter are presented in the book, and are a
model for other researchers and for the lay reader), he shows the
impact of such procedures on judgers and judged, and the alienation
from self that ensues for both. But in the same series of case studies
he also presents the vignette of Stanley, a 14-year-old boy, son of a
Polish worker, who is a true hero—perceptive far beyond his years;
competent in all he undertakes, including his studies, his relations
to adults, peers, and himself; skeptical yet warm; guarded yet open.
(I came across no such boy when, a dozen years ago, I searched for
autonomous youngsters in several public schools and several private
schools.) Stanley makes use of the high school, as Mr. Friedenberg
says, as if it were the Pennsylvania Railroad: he gets the services he

needs and wastes little time grumbling over inadequacies or internalizing the school's verdict on him. (Unlike the railroad, the school responds to Stanley and fully appreciates his qualities.)

Reflecting on Stanley, I wonder what the relevance is of the fact that he comes from the working class and has already, through the school, gained access to careers that will take him beyond his family (which he still respects). Does Stanley paradoxically have an easier time of self-definition because where he is and where he wants to be are dramatically distinct, and whatever he has done has been under his own steam? I cannot say: other working-class boys at the school were forced into alienation, and there are undoubtedly idiosyncratic qualities in Stanley which render him relatively immune to the prevalent viruses. But it is one implication of this book that, as the working class is drawn—by prosperity, mass culture, and national homogenization—increasingly into the lower-middle-class world of the school, the Stanleys will become even rarer than they now are.

How can alienation be overcome and (in Erich Fromm's term) relatedness be restored? Mr. Friedenberg believes that the high schools, even under present auspices, could take a firmer line in limiting their functions and interfere less in the total life of the teen-ager (granted that many interferences are animated by benevolence and not merely by fear of trouble). He would like to see the schools become more insistent about the authority of the mind—though this, I fear, could easily turn into another road to alienation in which the intellect, with its great powers of rationalization, becomes divorced from the tenderness which often appears so movingly with adolescence. And he would like to see the high schools confront the adolescent with continuous efforts at clarity in a humanistic curriculum which connects at one pole with the Western heritage and at the other with the students' own dilemmas. A large, and perhaps even at best an ambiguous, order. But none of it seems likely to be attained in a society which is itself amorphous, without a sense of mission in terms of which and against which a young person can define his own uniqueness and his own common humanity. Fortunately, outside of *Brave New World* with its artfully preserved Noble Savage, children have a tendency to grow into adolescents—even like Stanley—and thus to remind the rest of us, sometimes as painfully as this book does, of the extent to which we as adults have lost the "aristo-cratic" values of this stage. If adolescence does vanish in this coun-try, there is nothing—nothing, that is, but the very real danger of atomic or biological annihilation—to prevent its being reinvented.

David Riesman

BRATTLEBORO, VERMONT
JULY, 1959

The Vanishing Adolescent

Adolescence is not simply a physical process; there is more to it than sexual maturation. It is also—and primarily—a social process, whose fundamental task is clear and stable self-identification.

This process may be frustrated and emptied of meaning in a society which, like our own, is hostile to clarity and vividness. Our culture impedes the clear definition of any faithful self-image—indeed, of any clear image whatsoever. We do not break images; there are few iconoclasts among us. Instead, we blur and soften them. The resulting pliability gives life in our society its familiar, plastic texture. It also makes adolescence more difficult, more dangerous, and more troublesome to the adolescent and to society itself. And it makes adolescence rarer. Fewer youngsters really dare to go through with it; they merely undergo puberty and simulate maturity.

There has recently been growing concern about this; adults have noticed the change and gravely remark the emergence of a beat and silent generation. On the whole, we don't like it; and even those of us who find it a convenience would rather not be credited with having brought it about. Rather, we treat our silent, alienated, or apathetic youth as problems, as psychological or social aberrations from the normal course of adolescence. This evasion, however comforting, is unreal. It is the fully human adolescent—the adolescent who faces life with love and defiance—who has become aberrant.

Real adolescents are vanishing. I do not suppose they will become extinct, but they are certainly struggling to carry a disproportionate load of our common humanity. Many are holding back, and some are getting crushed. My purpose, in this book, is to show why this is so, and what I think we are losing.

Chapter I

ADOLESCENCE: *Self-Definition and Conflict*

One of the most precise clues to what is actually going on psychologically in a culture is its use of language. People only bother to name those aspects of their experience that mean something to them. Those who share the language, therefore, share to some extent a common situation and a common concern.

If a people have no word for something, either it does not matter to them or it matters too much to talk about. If they *do* have a word for something, it is worth asking why they have included in their concept just what they have, and not other aspects which might, from a slightly different point of view, easily have been included. And if they cannot use the words they have without becoming arch, coy, or diffuse—if they cannot discuss a subject of apparent importance to them with vigor and precision—they are clearly in some kind of trouble about it. When experience is deformed by conflict or anxiety, language no longer quite fits. The personal needs of those who are trying to discuss a problem come between their experience and their common symbols, and they find it difficult or impossible to speak about it normally.

Adolescence is one of the topics which is subject to all these difficulties and which is correspondingly difficult to discuss intelligibly in English. Despite our exaggerated concern for and almost prurient interest in the "teen-ager," we have no neutral term for persons between the ages of, say, fourteen and twenty-one. "Adolescent" has overtones at once pedantic and erotic, suggestive of primitive fertility rites and of the orgies of classical antiquity. "Young person" meets the requirements of British jurisprudence in referring precisely to a portion of this age range, but is too poor in connotations to be a useful phrase in ordinary speech. "Teen-ager" remains the choice for popular usage. It is patronizing, and sounds rather uneasy and embarrassed; but these qualities may add to its appeal, for many of us do indeed respond to adolescence with forced joviality.

There is no English noun which simply identifies precisely persons between the ages of fourteen and twenty-one, leaving the reader free to feel what he pleases about them. This is odd. We have neutral nouns for persons and things that arouse feeling in nearly everyone: child, adult, hangman, cancer, mother, mistress, senator. These are exact; they mean what they mean. They can be dissociated from their connotations if the context demands it. "Teenager" cannot be. What does one call an eighteen-year-old girl if one wishes to note that she has triumphed as Joan of Arc or Anne Frank, or written another successful novel? What does one call an eighteen-year-old boy in reporting that he has been killed in a training maneuver at boot camp? Such things do not happen to "teen-agers," absorbed as they are in delinquency and in endless telephone discussions of rock and roll.

Yet, if we have no convenient language for discussing adolescence we seem equally unable to dismiss it. And this too is rather odd. What is there about these eight or so years that lingers so in the psyche? Granted that puberty is a notable event, that the onset of sexual maturity and the bodily changes which ensue are dramatic, and that no language applies its word for "child" to persons beyond the early teens. Nothing so conspicuous demarcates the adolescent from the young adult; yet adults who are no longer young are likely to feel much more at ease with a young man of twenty-five than with a boy of eighteen. They place the two in different classes of humanity, while allotting thirty years, more or less, to middle age. These thirty years also bring changes in personality and body build, but we see them as gradual and have not divided them up with conceptual barriers.

This conception of an upper limit to adolescence is by no means universal. In most primitive cultures—variable as these are—young people are usually initiated into adult life shortly after puberty. They are conducted through *rites de passage* of varying degrees of harshness designed to "separate the men from the boys"; the separation is not a genuine period of adolescence but a brief *interregnum*. Essentially, in such societies, one is either a child or an adult, though adult society is marked by status differences quite as complex and elaborate as ours.

Adolescence is conceived as a distinct stage of life in societies so complicated and differentiated that each individual's social role and function takes years to define and learn. When years of special preparation for adult life are required, these years become a distinguishable period with its own rules, customs, and relationships. The ordeal of the classical British preparatory and public school, for example, could not simply be sweated out in a burst of adolescent pluck; the initiation became a way of life. To instill into youth the complex code of the empire-builder and gentleman so thoroughly that this would be maintained in loneliness and isolation, and even under conditions in which it had become something of a nuisance to all concerned, took time and more than time. It took experience, under discipline, in relating to many different kinds of people whose status with respect to oneself varied sharply. In this way, the schoolboy learned to respond with spontaneous and often deep personal feeling to some of the people and events in his life, while limiting the *range* of his response to persons and situations he had learned to regard as worth noticing.

The British public school, at its most imposing, made adolescence much more than an interregnum. It made it an epoch. Its austerity could be relieved by a sensitive husbanding of sparse human resources; its heroes became myths, and in turn clichés, but the schoolboy had strong feelings about them. The prefect who caned you for specific offenses might, at other times, offer brusque understanding when you seriously needed it. He might also be a sadistic bully, or simply a rather stupid boy who was good at games. There were classmates with whom you could share brief, vivid perceptions and long, comfortable silences, though there were many more with whom you could share nothing. There were masters who had some respect for scholarship and for boys, and there were others who respected neither. All these defined themselves through the years as individuals as well as parts of a system. They could be fought, but there was no getting away from them or erasing your experience with them. At best, they helped the adolescent make himself into a strongly characterized human being who was ready to go on to something more: at worst, their impact made adolescence interminable and their victims permanently fixated "old boys." In any case, they defined the content of adolescence; they gave the adolescent something to be adolescent about.

In a society that sets up special institutions for inducting the young into it, and takes several years doing it, the developmental process that we call adolescence can occur. This institutional provision need not, however, be formal or intentionally planned. A delinquent gang is such an institution. And even institutions as formal and coercive as the classical British public school or the old-fashioned military school influenced their students most strongly in ways that were not consciously planned, though they were certainly the consequence of powerful unconscious intentions.

The unconscious and conscious intentions that dominate a society are, of course, expressed through all its institutions, including those that deal with adolescents. The institutions which mold the adolescence of most young people in technically developed countries today are the instruments of a very different society from that which created the British public school or the military school. They are intended to yield young people predisposed to very different social behavior. They are seldom coercive or immediately painful, but rather informal, democratic, and apparently mild in operation. They make use of sanctions that hardly hurt at all when applied, but that often make their victims ill much later.

The kind of character these institutions—whether the school, the TV, or even the modern army and navy—tend to develop is in many ways the very opposite of that which the British public school, or the old-fashioned school of any kind, sought consciously and unconsciously to produce. All the contemporary institutions that bear on the young, diverse as they seem to be, are united in their insistence on cultivating sensitivity and pliability to the demands and expectations of other persons. Other-direction, adaptability, adjustment, conformity—call it what you will, the idea is familiar enough —is a trait of great short-run social usefulness in today's relatively open and rootless society; and that society has done a formidable job of creating institutions which mold other-directed and adjustable character structure.

One might expect that the general increase in blandness and good humor which has resulted would also have sweetened the relationship between adults and adolescents; and in many ways it has. There are real friendships between adolescents and adults in contemporary society, especially in America; it is taken for granted that there should be. This would not have been possible earlier, and it is still most unusual in many European or Latin-American countries. It is a basic development in human relations, scarcely less important than the simultaneous improvement in relations among different racial groups, which is resulting from quite similar social changes.

But the modern emphasis on cooperation and group adjustment has also injured the relationship between adolescents and adults in two very significant ways. These are not very widely recognized, but they lie, I believe, at the root of our difficulty in considering adolescence without self-consciousness or conflict. The first of these is rather superficial; the second is much more serious.

The tolerant, reasonable, democratic approach to "teen-agers"— like the comparable approach to formerly discriminated racial groups —is based on a premise of greater respect for them than the earlier attitude of coercive, if paternalistic, dominance. This much is valuable. But the same difficulty arises as in the improvement of inter-racial relations. In order for this to occur smoothly, the members of the dominant group must like and respect the subordinate group a good deal in the first place. If adults dislike or fear adolescents, the change will make those adults more frightened and more hostile, because it is a very real threat to their continued domination. In today's society they will probably have to be "nice to the kids" despite their fear and hostility; but they will most certainly try to maintain by seduction and manipulation the dominance they previously achieved by coercion and punishment.

This, it seems to me, is what usually does happen. Certainly, there are many exceptions, and the proportion seems to be growing nicely; but I think a detached observer of the behavior and attitudes of school personnel, juvenile court officials, and so forth would probably conclude that, on the whole, these individuals dislike and distrust youngsters more often than they like them. They are often disturbed at the prospect of being involved with young people in any situation that is not under their quite complete control; a dean who has grown accustomed to functioning as a rather fair-minded though rigid martinet is likely to become unscrupulous and con-spiratorial if changes in his school force him to act as "adviser" to an ostensibly self-governing student disciplinary committee. Such officials are usually willing to abandon coercive techniques of control in favor of manipulative ones, since these help them preserve a more favorable image of themselves as guides who are liked and accepted by their charges; and, in any case, manipulative techniques work better than coercive ones with modern youngsters, who are usually quite skilled themselves at making tyrants feel guilty. But the teacher, dean, or probation officer who genuinely sees youngsters as persons of dignity equal to himself and who is satisfied to have purely rational authority over them is still rather the exception. The point can be overstressed, and I do not mean to suggest that the planet has become a sort of Madison Avenue streamlined version of Dotheboy's Hall. But the perception of the orientation of the world of adults toward adolescents so well and movingly expressed by Holden Caulfield in *The Catcher in the Rye* seems to me almost wholly valid.

Much of the ambivalence of adults toward "teen-agers" is, I should judge, simply a kind of repressed panic-response to the liquidation of authority over them. It must be understood, however, that the loss of authority is real; the adult empire is tottering. All empires are; this is the era of skepticism about the relationship between authority and status. It is an error, I believe, to interpret what is happening as a decline in respect for authority as such. American youngsters today are generous in according respect to parents, teachers, and other adults who earn it as individuals; and they are far more perceptive of individual quality in their elders than they could possibly have been when all adults were regarded as potentially or actually hostile and dangerous. But it is true that they are less likely to respect an adult today simply because he occupies a position of authority. It is also true that a boy who can be punished for insulting you is far less frightening—even if he is *very* insulting—than a boy who offers out of sheer kindness to share his analyst with you because he has noticed, correctly, that you need help worse than he does.

Adults who do not basically like and respect adolescents—and this includes a large proportion of those who make a career of working with them—are badly frightened by the increasingly democratic relationships between adolescents and adults that are coming to prevail in our society. They have become more tense in their attitude toward youngsters, and contribute greatly to the difficulties of young people in our society. Their manipulative and covert hostility demoralizes adolescents and forms the basis of real personal and social problems. It is easier, and less damaging, for a youngster to face bad grades, disappointment at being passed over for a team or a club, or formal punishment, than it is for him to deal with gossip about his character or his manners, with teachers who pass the word along that he is a troublemaker or that he needs special patience and guidance because his father drinks.

Nevertheless, this is probably not too serious a matter, for it is pretty certain to work itself out in the course of time. Newer and better trained teachers and social workers tend to be of a somewhat different stamp. The youngsters themselves grow more accustomed to respectful handling and more confident of it; they become less rebellious but also less easily diverted from their own moral judgments and decisions. When they *do* nevertheless have to deal with a hostile or tricky adult, they are more likely to know what they want and what they are doing, and can face him coolly. He, in turn, is *not* really confident of himself or his authority, and rapidly becomes more anxious. He may stubbornly refuse to listen; he may lose his temper and really try to hurt them, and this time he may succeed. But he also finds that his efforts to dominate the young cause him more anxiety than he can easily bear. Unless his superiors support him in a counterattack, he is likely to withdraw gradually behind a barrage of indignant complaint. Ultimately, he becomes picturesque; the young may grow quite fond of him.

What is far more serious is that the emphasis on cooperation and group adjustment characteristic of modern life interferes specifically with the central developmental task of adolescence itself. *This task is self-definition. Adolescence is the period during which a young person learns who he is, and what he really feels. It is the time during which he differentiates himself from his culture, though on the culture's terms. It is the age at which, by becoming a person in his own right, he becomes capable of deeply felt relationships to other individuals perceived clearly as such.* It is precisely this sense of individuality which fails to develop, or develops only feebly, in most primitive cultures or among lower-status social groups. A successful initiation leads to group solidarity and a warm sense of belonging; a successful adolescence adds to these a profound sense of self—of one's own personality.

Personalization is the métier of adolescence. Of all persons, adolescents are the most intensely personal; their intensity is often uncomfortable to adults. As cooperation and group adjustment become pervasive social norms; as tolerance supersedes passion as the basis for social action; as personalization becomes false-personalization, adolescence becomes more and more difficult. Conceivably, it might become again a rather rare event, having no function in the new world of glad-handing primitives happy among their electronic trinkets. But, for the present at least, the old norms of individual character, personal devotion, particular love and hate retain enough authority to make those who remain faithful to them, as adolescents tend to do, extremely troublesome to their contemporaries.

Adolescents often behave much like members of an old-fashioned aristocracy. They maintain private rituals, which they often do not really understand themselves. They are extremely conservative in their dress and tastes, but the conventions to which they adhere are purely those of their own social group; they try to ignore the norms of the larger society if these conflict with their own. They can be extravagantly generous and extravagantly cruel, but rarely petty or conniving. Their virtues are courage and loyalty; while the necessity for even a moderate degree of compromise humiliates them greatly. They tend to be pugnacious and quarrelsome about what they believe to be their rights, but naïve and reckless in defending them. They are shy, but not modest. If they become very anxious they are likely to behave eccentrically, to withdraw, or to attack with some brutality; they are less likely to blend themselves innocuously into the environment with an apologetic smile. They are honest on occasions when even a stupid adult would have better sense.

They are therefore at a considerable disadvantage in many relationships of modern life. Modern life is hostile to the aristocratic social principle. Aristocratic attitudes and modes of action snarl its very mainsprings. They interfere with the conduct of practical affairs and impede administrative action. In busy, anxious, and ambitious people, they arouse anger and resentment; but beneath the anger and resentment there is shame and guilt.

Adolescents insult us by quietly flaunting their authenticity. They behave as if they did not even know that passion and fidelity are expensive, but merely assumed that everyone possessed them. This, certainly, is inexcusably valorous; and it is not excused. But it makes us awkward in their presence, and embarrassed in our approach to them.

Not all adolescents, by any means, retain this quality. There are many who learn to soothe adults ruffled by encounters with their more ardent and challenging peers, and charm them on suitable occasions by an ingratiating youthfulness. When a boy or girl is needed for display, they are available; in the same clothes all the others wear, they look a little—not too much—neater. Having them in charge of the school paper and the student government saves a good deal of wear and tear all around; they are described in their school records as having qualities of leadership.

At certain times and places—perhaps here and now—such boys and girls predominate. Processes comparable to natural selection almost insure that they will. Schools nudge them into the pathways believed to lead to success in adult life and rehearse them for it in carefully designed facsimiles of adult institutions. Student life in the modern high school is now conducted through a veritable rat-maze of committees. The big man on campus is a perfectly executed scale model of a junior executive. It may therefore seem either inconsistent or willfully sentimental that I have described my heuristic model of an adolescent as a knight in shining chino pants.

But I think it is valid to maintain this, not just because I have encountered a goodly few such errant defenders of the faith in the course of half a lifetime, but because I am concerned here with a process of growth rather than with a statistical norm. There is certainly no doubt that modern society has power to corrupt, and that it starts early. But the function of adolescence is growth and individuation, and these can be fruitful only if a reasonable and increasing degree of integrity is maintained.

A youngster who has abandoned the task of defining himself in dialectical combat with society and becomes its captive and its emissary may be no rarity; but he is a casualty. There is not much more to be said about him: one can only write him off and trust that the world will at least feed him well if it cannot keep him warm. The promise of maturity must be fulfilled by those who are strong enough to grow into it at their own rate as full bargaining members.

Must there be conflict between the adolescent and society? The point is that adolescence *is* conflict—protracted conflict—between the individual and society. There are cultures in which this conflict seems hardly to occur; but where it does not, the characteristic development of personality which we associate with adolescence does not occur either.

There are cultures, as in Margaret Mead's classic description of coming of age in Samoa, where the young pass delicately as Ariel through puberty into adulthood. But their peoples do not seem to us like adults; they are charming people, but they are from our point of view insufficiently characterized. There is not much difference between them, and they do not seem to make much difference to one another.

In other simple cultures, in which the role of the adult is likewise thoroughly familiar to the child by the time he reaches puberty, the young are initiated into adult life much more harshly. Sometimes the process is more loving than it appears to be, though the very fact that adults find it necessary to inflict it is conclusive evidence of some hostility toward the young. In any case, it is comparatively brief. Some of these cultures are primitive; others are relatively stable subcultures of the Western world like that of British coal miners whose sons are hazed into adult status by their elders when they first enter the mines themselves. But in these as well, the adults seem curiously indistinguishable by our criteria of personality. Differences of temperament and of attitude toward life may be very conspicuous indeed. But they stop short of what we regard as normal variation of human personality; the range is as wide, but not as deep.

And there are other cultures in which there is no conflict because conflict is thoroughly repressed. Not by externally applied brutality—this suppresses; it does not effectively repress. There are adolescents even in totalitarian countries, as the Polish and Hungarian authorities discovered in 1956. But where totalitarianism really sinks in, even the young will be so intensely anxious that no conflict will arise. Only those feelings and attitudes approved by society will then even occur to them as possibilities. There can be no adolescence in *1984*.

Conflict between the individual and society, as Lionel Trilling has so clearly stated in *Freud and the Crisis of Our Culture*,* is inherent in the development of personality by the standards of Western man. Freud is still the source of our most tough-minded psychodynamic system, and this point is basic to it. And it is in adolescence that this conflict is critical to individual development. Or to put it another way, and perhaps more truly, adolescence *is* this conflict, no matter how old the individual is when it occurs. Adolescent conflict is the instrument by which an individual learns the complex, subtle, and precious difference between himself and his environment. In a society in which there is no difference, or in which no difference is permitted, the word "adolescence" has no meaning.

But conflict is not war; it need not even involve hostile action. It must, to be sure, produce some hostile feelings, among others. But there need be no intent to wound, castrate, or destroy on either side. Conflict between the adolescent and his world is dialectical, and leads, as a higher synthesis, to the youth's own adulthood and to critical participation in society as an adult. Some of the experiences of adolescence which turn out to be most beneficial to growth are, it is true, painful at the time. Looking for your first job, among strangers; learning that your first love is the girl she is but not the girl you need; getting soundly beaten in your first state-wide track meet when you are used to being the fastest runner in town—none of this is fun. But such experiences are not sickening, heartbreaking, or terrifying because, even at the time, they can be felt as bringing you in closer touch with reality. The pain they produce is somehow accepted as benign, like soreness following unaccustomed physical exercise or the pain of normal childbirth. Growth is more satisfying, and far more reassuring, than comfort; though normal growth is comfortable most of the time.

One cannot, therefore, use the inevitability of conflict in adolescence as a justification for actions which hurt adolescents on the pretext of "toughening them up." If "growing pains" are never sicken-

* Boston: The Beacon Press, 1955.

ing, heartbreaking, or terrifying, it is equally true that heartbreak, terror, and a sense of insult and violation contribute nothing to growth. They stunt it or twist it, and the grower is more or less deformed. Perhaps the commonest deformation which these cause in persons too young to know how to handle themselves in pain is apathy.

In their encounters with society, youngsters are frequently badly hurt, and there is no mistaking this kind of agony for growing pains. They are sickened and terrified; they feel their pride break, cringe from the exposure of their privacy to manipulation and attack, and are convulsed with humiliation as they realize that they cannot help cringing and that, in fact, their responses are now pretty much beyond their control. Control once regained is consolidated at a less humane level; there will be no more love lost or chances taken on the adversary.

A number of psychological and social dynamisms can take over at this juncture; none of them is a part of the process of healthy growth, though some at least give time for scars to form so that growth may be resumed later. But most of these defense mechanisms are dangerous in their total context, although they make perfectly good sense in the light of the victim's immediate emotional condition. This is the fundamental dilemma of organism. A severe heart attack is not such a bad idea from the immediate viewpoint of the exhausted heart, if only the rest of the body and the heart itself, as a muscle, were not so thirsty for blood. Somehow, however it has been insulted, the heart must be kept in action, for its own sake as well as for that of the body as a whole; though a wise physician knows when to keep demands on it to a minimum, and also knows that the minimum may still be more than can be borne.

Growth, too, must continue. Apathy, a fawning acceptance of authority, or a hard-eyed campaign of organized delinquency with enough real violence to show you mean business, may all be understood as functional for adolescents bearing certain kinds of wounds. But understandable or not, functional or not, these are dangerous expedients for the young. They may provide cover for the processes of healing, and facilitate the formation of strong emotional scar tissue. But they not only lead to more trouble with society; they lead away from the kinds of relationships by which growth continues, and from the kind of self-perception of which growth consists.

Delinquency, apathy, and seductive fawning are not aspects of the essential conflict between youth and society which constitutes adolescence. They are the consequences of the conflict having gone terribly wrong, and a corresponding wisdom and patience—more than is usually available under actual working conditions—are needed to restore it as a fruitful process. For most young people, of course, things do not go terribly wrong. They go moderately wrong, but we nevertheless grow up, more or less, and conduct ourselves toward the next generation in its need with such humanity as we can muster. For the result, no blame attaches. Adam and Eve, at the time that Cain was born, had no opportunity to read the works of Gesell.

I know of no reason to suppose that, at the present time, there is a crisis in our relationship to youth; and, in any case, this is certainly not a book of instructions to be supplied with adolescents. But if the function of adolescence is self-definition, one would expect it to be very difficult in a society which suffers from a dearth of individuality and in which alienation is a crucial problem. And if the instrument of self-definition is the conflict between the adolescent and a basically humane society—which nevertheless has purposes of its own, and more to do than take care of kids—one would expect the self-defining process to break down as that society became less humane and more manipulative. A society which has *no purposes* of its own, other than to insure domestic tranquillity by suitable medication, will have no use for adolescents, and will fear them; for they will be among the first to complain, as they crunch away at their benzedrine, that tranquilizers make you a square. It will set up sedative programs of guidance, which are likely to be described as therapeutic, but whose apparent function will be to keep young minds and hearts in custody till they are without passion.

We have by no means gone so far as yet; but the sort of process of which I speak is already discernible. In this extended essay, I hope to analyze the social processes bearing on adolescence as these show themselves in the social institution officially responsible for their nurture—the school. It will also be necessary to examine the processes of personal and emotional growth fundamental to adolescence, so that we may come to an understanding of what it means to a young person, called a "teen-ager," to try to grow into individual adulthood under the conditions of contemporary life.

Chapter II

EMOTIONAL DEVELOPMENT IN ADOLESCENCE

Two aspects of growth that contribute most to a clear self-definition are climactic in adolescence. One of these is the capacity for tenderness toward other persons. Since tenderness is fired by sexuality and expresses a primarily sexual feeling, adults are not astonished that it should appear very strongly in the emotional spectrum of adolescence. But we are inclined to underestimate the power and the human value of adolescent love. For one thing, it frightens us and sometimes makes us more envious than we know. For another, we live in a culture which sentimentalizes children and therefore tends to lose sight of the contrasting capacity for tenderness that adolescence brings. Finally—and for reasons which we must subsequently examine rather closely—we regard many of the things and persons beloved by adolescents, including other adolescents, with scorn and utter contempt and so disregard the feeling they arouse. Adolescents tend to be passionate people, and passion is no less real because it is directed toward a hot-rod, a commercialized popular singer, or the leader of a black-jacketed gang. Our exploitive mass culture makes it terribly hard for youngsters to find or even to identify appropriate objects for love; but it is the new power of adolescence to weave tenderness into the fabric of personality that produces a pattern of life not wholly cynical or expedient.

The other major development is an attitude of respect for competence. Adults often find it hard to see this in adolescent behavior, partly because they lack respect for and disapprove of the kind of competence the adolescent is seeking and partly because adolescent competence tends now to be tapped off for commercial purposes and standardized before it has had much chance to develop or to contribute to the development of the adolescent. But respect for competence in oneself and others is crucial in adolescence, for it is crucial to self-definition. In a world as empirical as ours, a youngster who does not know what he is good *at* will not be sure what he is good *for*; he must know what he can do in order to know who he is.

The things he does well may not, of course, be things that win him the esteem of the community; some adolescents, when they get nervous and upset, steal cars and take joy rides in them the way an adult might work off his mood by gardening or a game of golf. But they must be skills that identify him to himself and others, and keep him from getting lost.

In order to understand in detail how tenderness and competence are involved in adolescent growth, we must first establish a basis for interpreting personality development in adolescence as a general process. Because adolescent personality, especially under American social conditions, is so much affected by the feelings and relationships youngsters establish among themselves, I believe that the psychoanalytic system developed by Harry Stack Sullivan and his school will be more useful than the classical Freudian schema. I shall draw freely on Sullivan's work—particularly the *Interpersonal Theory of Psychiatry*.*

Sullivan distinguishes two stages of childhood between infancy and adolescence. By "childhood" he refers only to the *first* of these. He considers as a *child* only a person so young that most of his experience occurs in the home. His interpersonal relations are almost entirely with members of his family. Unlike the infant, he has clear interpersonal relations, in that he can consistently tell one person from another and expects different things from them; but these persons all share his essentially private world. They are not strangers, and at this age he does not see them as competitors. As soon as he does—that is, as soon as he begins to approach others expecting to find them impersonal and bent on their own aims to his possible disadvantage—childhood is at an end. When this will be is not a matter of biological age or individual psychodynamics. Childhood ends earlier in lower class, where children may have to fend for themselves almost as soon as they can walk, than it does in middle class. It ends earlier in this country, with our emphasis on early self-reliance and getting along with others, than in France, where

* New York: Norton, 1953. Precisely because Sullivan treats human development in a context of specific social experience, he is less widely applicable than Freud to cultures different from our own. But for just this reason he is more helpful to us in following the emotional development of adolescents in America.

sometimes only sex is strong enough to force parents to recognize childhood's end.

Later childhood, or roughly what Freud called the *latency period*, Sullivan speaks of as the *juvenile era*. The juvenile era begins when social institutions oblige the child to deal *as an individual* with the problems of his relationship to strangers, with the cumulative difficulties that arise from the difference between what he sees in himself and what they see in him, what he needs and what they have to give, what he gives and what they can accept. Sullivan's juvenile, it must be stressed, is *pre-adolescent*; he is not the juvenile of Juvenile Delinquency. He is the youngest person whose fate depends on his ability to communicate with people who have little share in his life, and who are more interested in themselves than in what he is trying to tell them about himself.

Sullivan sees the child as primarily engaged in building concepts which are general enough to permit intelligible communication with other persons. The private symbol system which the infant builds for himself must be modified to permit other persons to understand him; he must consent to a relationship between his language and external phenomena which is fairly consistent with the rules observed in the outer world; he cannot go on calling everything that has fur and moves "doggy." Since these rules are not so important, really, to any of us as our own view of the meaning of our experience, a good deal is lost in the process; but a good deal is gained in not becoming psychotic, which is the other choice. The child learns to talk about what he perceives; that is, he learns to make roughly the same sound other members of his family make to denote similar situations, or at least to say the same thing consistently in response to the same situation. Some of us go through life saying "I'm hungry!" when we mean "Nobody loves me!"; but we say it with as much conviction at three hundred pounds as we did at thirty.

For the fundamental, underlying feeling-tone—aroused in the infant as a crude response to feeling and perception, and coloring much of his subsequent response to all of life—there is no language; and Sullivan views the most important experiences of life as being permanently incommunicable in language. But between sensitive individuals, feeling is communicated with great precision by empathy, as it was initially from the mother to the infant before the infant had any language.

Neither childhood nor the juvenile era, as Sullivan presents them, does much to advance beyond infancy our capacity for empathy, for precision of *emotional* response; indeed, there is likely to be retrogression. The child who says there are big rats in the alley and gets spanked for lying the third time he says it learns something about how adults use language and the importance they attach to it. He learns what a spanking is and what a rat is not; all this is presumably useful knowledge to take along on the solitary journey toward maturity. But he does not learn, and neither do his parents, what he meant when he said there were rats in the alley. This gets plowed under.

The important point is not that we learn to talk in childhood, but that we learn to repress meanings that are not subject to consensual validation; we learn to keep quiet about what other people cannot see. There are privileged occasions, of course, when storytelling is different from lying; but the discipline of having to distinguish them reinforces the importance of the distinction. And it is not, of course, primarily a matter of the discipline of formal speech by formally imposed sanction. It is rather that we learn in childhood to sacrifice emotional vividness to intellectual cogency. Both learning and inhibition are involved. The process is necessary; but in blasting wide gateways through the walls of our private world, inscriptions of great significance are obliterated.

And through these gateways, during the juvenile era, the world pours in hordes of Mongolian ferocity and sometimes Mongolian idiocy. To a degree hardly paralleled in what we regard as primitive cultures, which may live by rules of exquisite courtesy, life among juveniles in America is life in the raw. To find anything like it one would have to turn, not to the upper Amazon, but to a prison or a lunatic asylum; that is to say, to a place of resort for individuals whose peculiar distinction is that they are *not* socialized and have little regard for or perception of one another. Juveniles deal with each other with a crudity unparalleled in later life. It is not altogether terrifying if one is a little savage oneself, but a juvenile group is no place for sensitivity. We are inclined as a people to be highly sentimental about children; but I think most thoughtful adults, if they were obliged to sojourn among American eight-to-ten-year-olds, would want to be awfully careful which side of Alice's mushroom they nibbled.

Groups of juveniles are not friendly; and strongly felt friendships do not commonly form among them, though there is often constant association between members of juvenile cliques. They are not there to be friendly; they are there to work out a crude social system and to learn the ropes from one another. To some extent they behave like the gang in an office, jockeying for position within a superficially amiable social group. But if—as seems unlikely—there is still to be found among literate Americans an individual who regards sex as the source of viciousness in human affairs, I would urge him to compare the human relations existing within a juvenile clique to those usually found among adolescents and simply to note what sexual maturation can contribute in a few years to increased sensitivity and tenderness for other persons. Relations *within* the clique, that is, relations between it and the external world, are another matter.

But precisely because of its crudity, the juvenile experience contributes greatly to increased mental cogency, accelerating the processes begun in childhood. It is frank. Juvenile appraisals of other juveniles make up in clarity what they lack in charity; those not too sensitive can learn a great deal about themselves which they would never have learned at home. Juvenile jokes are frank filth cast in the form of jokes as a stratagem to prevent adults—who are terrified of having no sense of humor—from washing the mouth out with soap; but they are explicit and detailed and a welcome relief from the euphemisms of the middle-class bathroom. Juvenile politics is dirty; but it works, and it cuts interfering adults bent on prissiness down to something less than size if they venture beyond their sphere of proper authority.

The juvenile era provides the solid earth of life; the security of having stood up for yourself in a tough and tricky situation; the comparative immunity of knowing for yourself just exactly how the actions that must not be mentioned feel; the safety of knowing the exact margin by which adults are stronger, smarter, or trickier than you; the calm, gained from having survived among comrades, that makes one ready to have friends. You learn a lot being a juvenile.

But in the process it would seem that such vestiges of creative subjectivity as may have survived childhood must certainly be eradicated permanently.* So they often are; most of us have lost whatever capacity for poetry we may once have had. In the juvenile era, as that is experienced in the ambience of the American public school, most children will certainly learn to feel severe anxiety at the eruption of any manifestation of their inner life. The eight-year-old who cries, or gives in to a sudden impulse to kiss the teacher, the ten-year-old who uses language differently from his peers—each faces an avalanche of derision. The attack he incurs may be spontaneous; it may also be structured by the teacher as a teaching device or a way of controlling the class. A recent paper† describes in sober detail but with lurid effectiveness the specific processes by which the feeling and originality expressed in children's stories and use of language are stamped out in elementary school. The appalling element in his observations is the relentless glee with which these juveniles attack one another with what Henry calls "carping criticism"—the intense competitive delight with which they catch one another out. The teachers, being good agents of their culture, encourage this, but they do not have to encourage it much. Henry reports how a teacher, seeing an element of genuine literary quality in a youngster's work, tried to arrest the flow of criticism and mockery long enough to point it out. She was not able to. The difficulty appeared to stem less from the actual hostility of the juveniles than from their inability to comprehend that the teacher's purpose had become momentarily constructive, though they had by this time become highly adept at sensing what kind of response she wanted and giving it to her.

Interpersonal denigration is not, of course, exclusively juvenile. It is rawest among juveniles, unrestrained by either tenderness or

* Cf. Ernest G. Schachtel, "On Memory and Childhood Amnesia," *A Study of Interpersonal Relations*, Patrick Mullahy (ed.) (New York: Hermitage Press, 1949; Thomas Nelson & Sons, successors).

† Jules Henry, "Attitude Organization in Elementary School Classrooms," *American Journal of Orthopsychiatry*, XXVIII, No. 1 (January, 1957), 117-33.

sophistication; but it continues through adolescence and for many adults seems to constitute the major source of satisfaction in life. But in adolescence other kinds of interpersonal relations become rather common as well, and among many adolescent groups become dominant. Adolescents jockey for position, pride themselves on knowing their way around, compete bitterly, and play dirty. But they often do much more.

In adolescence, other people begin to make a difference as individuals rather than as sources of support or obstructions to impulse. Shortly before the physical onset of puberty, a different quality of feeling suffuses one's perception of certain other individuals. They are loved.

Children and juveniles do not love, in this sense, because they are rarely interested in the complete personalities of other persons. Their concern is limited to what affects them; as long as their lives run according to custom, they do not care much what other people are really like. Within this area of concern their perception is acute and their judgment sound; children are traditionally known to be all but impossible to fool by cant or hypocrisy. Empathy stands them in good stead in detecting the real predispositions of others toward them. *The Pied Piper,* with its mass deception, is one of the few classical nursery tales which is really silly.

But their penetrating intuition does not permit children to form complete human relationships, since they take no interest in the totality of other persons. Richard Hughes' classic *The Innocent Voyage* (also called *High Wind in Jamaica*), which tells how a group of children cause a band of pirates, who kidnap but do not otherwise harm them, to be hanged as murderers, is not silly at all. The pirates grow to love the children; the children like the pirates. But there is friction; the children get out of hand and are punished occasionally; and in the end they perjure themselves at the pirates' trial because they see no reason for distinguishing between reality and the complex fantasies with which they have been assuaging their feelings. They regard the pirates as friends, more or less; they know that they have been treated as well as the pirates' resources permitted; and they know, more or less, that their testimony is misleading and that it will cause these men's death. But the innocent voyage is over; and the pirates, as individuals, have less interest or value for them than the new melodrama of the trial, which they play out to the hilt.

Children give of themselves freely and have much to give; their feeling and spontaneity are a constant delight to adults. But they hardly love even their parents, much as they need them and however comforting they find them. They see parents as an indispensable institution, not as whole persons. This leads to affection, trust, and loyalty. Love is rounder and more precise.

It begins, and begins with some intensity, in early adolescence. It begins in loving someone *other* than oneself and finishes, if one is fortunate, in loving someone *different* from oneself—as different as man is from woman. The passionate attachments of earliest adolescence are between chums of the same sex. Whether anything sexual happens in the course of them is unimportant, unless someone steps in and makes it important. Indeed, it is largely a matter of definition, though some of the feelings these youngsters arouse in each other are certainly erotic.

Sullivan attributes great developmental value to these attachments of early adolescence. Far from presaging homosexuality in later life, they are notably absent from the case histories of adult homosexuals—a finding expressed also in somewhat different language some years ago by Lewis Terman* in his study of *Sex and Personality*. It is evidently much easier to lose oneself in dreams of golden youths if one lacks intimate knowledge of real boys of the kind that only another boy can share. Homophilic love, if not essential to ultimate heterosexual love, certainly tends to pave the way toward it and enrich it.

It does so by restoring a measure of trust in feeling, and combining this with more precise self-perception. Children and juveniles are self-centered; early adolescents, increasingly able to take others to heart, still find this easier at first if the other is not different enough to be threatening. Tenderness, when it is unfamiliar, makes us shy; and shyness dominates relationships with persons beyond our experience; if they are also shy, as girls are in early adolescence, the friendship is likely to be stillborn. Between chums of early adolescence, only tenderness itself is strange.

With love comes trust, which leads to mutual exploration

* Lewis M. Terman and Catherine Cox Miles, *Sex and Personality* (New York: McGraw-Hill, 1936), p. 320.

and the confidence to accept intrusion. The feeling of chums in early adolescence for each other is usually their first experience of unconditional acceptance by another person. Once this is established, the two can learn about themselves from each other without the tension of the juvenile proving ground. The learning goes deeper, providing a warm and healing light by which old wounds are examined and old and crumbling defenses abandoned.

This is a genuine therapeutic experience of unique value. Parents cannot help their children in this way, for they are too much involved in the situation which has brought about whatever damage has occurred; if it is severe, the children are quite aware that imprudent self-revelation may lead to further pain and rejection. Children and juveniles cannot help each other in this way; their relationships are too ambivalent and too incomplete. But Tom, at the age of thirteen or fourteen, can say to Dick: "Why do you always have to be such a big wheel?" or "You don't really feel that way any more; you're just trying to make something out of it!" or "That was pretty stupid, what we pulled in school yesterday!" or even just "Well, if that's how you feel about it, screw you, Bud!" And Dick will listen to Tom, when he could hardly afford to listen to anybody else.

Dick does not have to compete with Tom; and he does not have to please him. Their commitment to each other has already been made, without any reservation or purpose of evasion. This is not to say that the friendship between them will run smoothly; it certainly will not and would be less useful if it did. Tom and Dick will fight and bear each other's wounds. Their job is not to be nice to each other, but to be real to each other.

If they are, if there are no traumatic betrayals or intercessions, Dick and Tom help each other very much. Each learns how good it feels to care about another person. Each learns much more about himself from the other; each learns that what makes the other supremely valuable to him is his *difference* from himself. Each confirms the other in masculine self-imagery; each is now ready to risk greater differences for the sake of even greater rewards. The focus of attention shifts. By this time, Dick and Tom are about ready to take Jane and Alice to a high-school dance, though for the first year or so they may all prefer to double-date.

If Jane and Alice are also ready to be real, the exploration and self-definition which tenderness makes possible continue in depth. Dick learns that his relationship to Jane is not a conquest but a process. As they become men and women the process becomes more complex and richer; more is involved, more is constructed, more is maintained. In mature love between adults the process of self-definition, and clarification of the meaning of life and of one's place in it, continues and becomes more abstract. But the basis of this process remains courage to be oneself in all one's imperfection, sustained by a measure of unconditional tenderness; and this is the basis on which Tom and Dick began it together.

Despite the attention it has received, the exact role of sex in this still seems unclear and confused. In view of the amount of study that has gone into it, I cannot but believe that the terms on which we approach such questions are what preclude our getting sensible answers. We certainly know that the response of human beings to one another is not easily compartmentalized. We are all animals, and placental mammals at that; but not much insight is gained by trying to classify our feelings or behavior into the erotic and the nonerotic. In considering adolescence, sexuality must be regarded in somewhat the same light as photosynthesis in the study of ecology—as the penultimate source of all energy. It cannot be denied that weeds are often a lot better at it than useful domestic plants, and that they look it; it is because they regard photosynthesis as an end in itself that weeds never get anywhere. But the process is benign, and it seems fortunate that it can be carried on successfully under so wide a variety of circumstances.

In adolescence, boys and girls do, I think, respond with quite different emotions to the erotic elements in a situation, though much of this difference is culturally determined. I am not here referring to their experiences as lovers, which must obviously be different. I mean that in our society boys and girls seem to react differently to situations which are not themselves sexual but which arouse a partially erotic response. I think, too, that the way in which boys and girls differ is not what the masculine and feminine stereotypes have led us to expect. Boys, for example, seem to me usually more concerned with their appearance than girls and also to have more idea what they actually look like and how other people will respond to the way they look. Our image of a beautiful girl is so rigidly defined and constantly reiterated by every medium of communication that it has become in a sense highly impersonal. Not every girl can be beautiful; but even a girl who is gets less credit for it than she deserves. It is always a little like seeing the Riviera; however breathtaking the effect, one's very first response is that it looks exactly the way it is supposed to, and that one has seen it before. Girls, therefore, are likely to approach beauty as if it were an effect to be achieved,—not an *artificial* effect but still an *external* one—the invocation of a social norm which exists altogether independently of themselves. And their attitude toward the result is likely to be quite detached. A vain young woman is, in my experience, rare.

Boys, in contrast, are often very vain; and their vanity is very personal; if they are handsome, they think of their handsomeness as peculiarly their own. They dress for it specifically, not according to social norms; a well-built, sun-bronzed boy will fight like a tiger to keep his mother from getting him out of his torn T-shirt and Ivy League pants with the useful buckle in the back, and into a conservative suit designed to conceal his fearful symmetry. Boys seem to get a different kind of satisfaction than girls from response to their physical attractiveness. Girls, I believe, are likely to find admiration for their beauty stimulating—not in the erotic sense, but as an awareness that physical attraction may open avenues to a variety of interesting relationships and experiences; they become more alert. Boys seem to become less alert; they bask in physical regard like alligators on a log. Provided there is no seductive purpose behind the response they arouse—and this they are very quick to sense and resent —it seems to reassure them, and they get sleepy.

There is also, I think, a fairly consistent sex difference in emotional stability in adolescence; again my observations contradict the stereotype. Boys seem on the whole to be moodier, more intense, more mystical almost. The next time you go to a basketball game watch the faces of the players as well as the play. You will see few expressions of recognizable emotion; hardly anyone ever smiles; displays of anger are more frequent, but usually occur during timeouts. What one sees instead are moments of ecstasy and transfiguration, when the player seems as wholly concentrated within his perception of his function as a Hindu holy man. Players are trained for this, of course; but training must be suited to the kind of response of which they are capable, and adolescent boys are capable of just this piercing intensity. Of all sports, basketball seems most suited to their physical and emotional status: the tempo, which demands speed and endurance rather than crushing power; the ritual maze of regulations and penalties, carrying the definition of fair play to obsessive lengths; even the affectionate slaps on the bottom by which coaches and teammates support and reassure a player in a critical situation.

Girls also play a form of basketball, of course, as do paraplegics in wheel chairs and, for all I know, purple cows; but I do not know why. Even a culture which can usually convince itself that it would enjoy nothing more than the opportunity to observe scantily clad young ladies closely for two or three hours seems to find something incongruous in the spectacle and to avoid it. The emotional aura seems wrong; a girls' basketball team is likely to strike an audience as *unconvincing*, in the same sense that a bad play does, even if it is technically competent. Dr. Johnson might have compared a girl playing basketball to a woman preacher.

Boys seem nearly always to be better at games; they take them much more seriously, and learn to control their anxieties in serious situations by treating them as if they were games; how WAAFs must have hated RAF slang! When girls take something seriously, as Judith did Holofernes and Juliet marriage, they are not likely to regard it as a game; they do not play fair; they do not play. This is not absence of humor but presence of mind; humor is not expended on jokes but reserved for use as a commentary on the meaning of more complete situations. The stereotype of women as weaker and less stable emotionally than men seems to be based on the hysteria and irresponsibility that were the only rational and effective attacks that could be made against the Victorian father and husband and his equivalent at other times and places. In the absence of male domination and authoritarianism, these phenomena are not observed.

We do observe silly adolescent girls; bobby-soxers are more ridiculous than the leather-jacket lads to whom they attach themselves. But they are silly partly through self-parody; this is the willful, essentially controlled, annoying silliness of the Shakespearean fool faithful to his master even unto the blasted heath. Certainly the Fool is foolish enough; but what adjective can we then apply to Lear? Yet

Lear is very like a delinquent boy in the feelings he expresses and in the way he ruins himself—in his fatal confusion about the relationship between authority, responsibility, and love. Had the Fool been less foolish, Lear would not have let him stay by his side. Whether the leather-jacketed boy is worth the sacrifice is a question on which the bobby-soxer's judgment is likely to be sounder than ours. Her decision may be costly, but it will not be silly.

It is not likely to be self-destructive. Heterosexual love—the completion of the process of learning to cherish another for his difference from oneself and for the sake of what T. S. Eliot called "the new person—us!" *—has its own healing power. *"Un certo balsamo,"* Zerlina called it, promising that it would heal all the bruises Don Giovanni had inflicted on Masetto's poor, beat-up limbs and trunk, "if the rest is sound!" For Don Giovanni himself, incapable of love or of response to it, there was no balsam.

But adolescence cannot be understood simply as an exercise in the development of tenderness. Other processes continue. Adolescence is distinguished from earlier stages of development by the warp of tenderness; but the tough fibers of social experience continue, as in the juvenile era, to tie the personality together. In the modern, knowledgeable adolescent, alert to the expectations of his peers and of adults, they may quite dominate the pattern. Little designs that look like affection will doubtless be worked into the fabric—or, on the mass-produced article, printed—but they will not be a part of the weave. Sometimes the personality is not woven from love and experience, but seems to have been knitted from one long, cool skein of know-how. The result is wonderfully silky and appealing, and conforms to every indicated contour, but it does not wear very well. One snag, and there is a tendency to run.

Living among other adolescents, in the peer-group, decisively influences the developing fabric of personality. Strength, vividness, richness of pattern, warmth and crush-resistance are all necessary to a good life with others. It is also helpful if occasional stains can be removed without permanent weakening or discoloration. Each of these properties depends on a proper relationship of social competence and realism to emotional responsiveness and sensitivity. In

* In *The Cocktail Party*, Act II (New York: Harcourt, Brace, 1950), p. 137.

the adolescent peer-group that relationship may be developed toward the end of personal autonomy.

The social dynamics of the adolescent peer-group are continuations of those of the juvenile era; there is no sudden shift or sharp break. But they become subtler and less crude. The group undertakes more complex activities; a wider variety of different kinds of competence proves to be useful; greater alertness in detecting and accepting them in otherwise unpromising individuals pays off. An odd and cranky boy who can nevertheless write an editorial for the school paper so skillfully that embarrassed authority can find no grounds for censorship is not now the butt of ridicule; he is a prize. It is worth a good deal of effort to keep him, and keep him out of trouble; and it takes a good deal of skill. The ugly, rather taciturn girl who with fifty dollars can decorate the gymnasium for a school dance so skillfully that the Persian Room, by comparison, looks a little too Persian does not have to be able to attract partners when the dance takes place—does not have to want to; she is *in*. The pudgy boy who can actually cook finds that young couples are hungry after the dance is over; he is in, too.

There is even more maneuvering than among juveniles. But much more is at stake; more refined technique pays off. It is no longer enough to compete loudly for success in a favored teacher's classroom. Accurate appraisals must be made of individual teachers' qualities, demands, and weakness. These appraisals must be *right*; they cannot be undertaken as carelessly as a translation or a lab report. A fraternity house must keep files of examinations if it is to provide its members with reliable support in emergencies; and these must be acquired without incident, without clumsiness.

Perception must be continuously refined. Teachers cannot be classified into bad guys and good guys; there are good teachers who are bad guys, and after six months they are more tolerable than bad teachers who are good guys. There are good teachers who are good guys who are troublesome nevertheless, because they are guilty about being good for the wrong reasons.

Within the peer-group, power and influence can be tasted, and adolescents quickly develop a gourmet's palate. There is a difference between influence and authority, though they are often vested in the same individual; but when they are not, power is more likely to be found on the side of influence, and authority will manage to manage. But influence does not mean pushing people around; it means leading them to want to do what you want them to do. The more influence you have, the easier this gets, until you couldn't stop them; an influential sorcerer has many devoted apprentices. But influence is not sorcery; it requires real awareness of what other people need and some skill in helping them get it. More than anything else, it requires a clear understanding of what is going on and of how things actually work. An influential person is no bully; he is a sculptor who works in the medium of human situations. He must respect his tools, his materials, and his market.

The social system of adolescence is no longer crude. Socialization within the peer-group engenders acute perception of how individuals behave and shrewd insight into their needs and motives. It develops in the adolescent a very wide field of view. Adolescents are cliquish and clannish, but they are not usually smug and parochial; almost any youngster except a member of a hostile clique or gang can be considered for acceptance and inclusion on his merits if his qualifications are needed. Almost any well-disposed adult may find that he has been identified and designated to serve as resource person, ally, informal therapist, and diplomat and mediator if conflict gets out of hand.

Adolescent judgments of what other individuals can and will do for, to, or with them are usually both sound and stable. The mistakes they make are generally due to an inability to take account of factors that are beyond their experience, though an adult might have been wary of them. They probably will not clearly understand, for example, the relationship between a high-school principal and the pillars of the community who determine the policies of the board of education. They will not easily spot the less familiar character disorders in a classmate or teacher—and may seriously misjudge what he will do if the situation alters. But within the limits imposed by their inexperience they are sharp.

What differentiates their judgment most from that of the juvenile is the tremendous value adolescents place on *competence*. Competence is the foundation of autonomy; in the adolescence peer-group it is respected in a variety of forms. Respect for competence is a penetrating source of discipline. In adolescence it is almost a religion, and sometimes more; I have known adolescents who had become atheists, not because they did not believe in God, but because they did, and were disgusted with the way He handled His job. Social sensitivity that is alert to competence and that bases its distinctions upon it cannot become merely snobbish or other-directed. Adolescent groups have a certain immunity to these vices, though not enough to resist them forever in a culture in which they are endemic.

The first annual Newport Jazz Festival (1954) illustrated adolescent attitudes toward competence quite clearly. It was a moving experience, and in many ways a unique one. About three-quarters of the audience appeared to be adolescent and, from the accents and snatches of overheard conversation, mostly from the greater exurban area which stretches from Mercersberg to Andover. Even these youngsters do not always have money; and Newport in any case did not have rooms; so most seemed to be sleeping in the cars they had come in for the two or three nights of the Festival. Yet this is the only audience I can recall in which the younger people were in the expensive seats and the older folk in the cheap ones.

During the entire two days I saw no single example of eccentric dress or behavior, or of exhibitionism—not even of excessive rapture or devotion. Here was none of the intensity of basketball; the occasion did not demand it. But it was serious in the way I should suppose a cabinet meeting would be serious at a time when there was no special crisis. These people knew what they were there for, and they knew what they expected.

They got it, too; even without knowing much about jazz, you could tell that. With one exception, none of the musicians put on a show. The brief introductory presentations were models of casual dignity and wit; Mr. Kenton never spoke as to the celebrants of an arcane mystery; he never got folksy; he never talked down. Good jazzmen do not; probably half the trouble adults have with "teen-agers" would never arise if schoolmen had the same understanding. Throughout the second evening of the Festival, for about five hours, it either drizzled or poured, and the seats were in the open. This was an inconvenience; but the concert went ahead as planned. The bandshell was covered, and the music was good. The audience stayed where it was.

Against this, to be honest, one must surely weigh in the balance the response of American youth to its sorry succession of Elvises. This is a cause for concern; but not, I think, for condemnation of adolescents. Few members of any community can survive saturation bombing, and the communications industries subject the "teen-ager" to little else. As a singer, Elvis has technical virtues, but as a social phenomenon, he is not pretty; and he does reflect the taste of the American adolescent in large numbers. But he does not reflect their free choice. Our Elvises are an infant industry, protected by the major radio, phonograph and television companies from the competition of more specialized appeals. Doubtless, nothing better could appeal to as many "teen-agers" at once. But what is needed to foster the development of autonomy during adolescence is not something better that would appeal to as large a number of youngsters. Instead, a large number of different artistic resources are needed; each more meaningful, and each satisfied to appeal to a small number of adolescents who are able, because of the special circumstances of their individual lives, to find it meaningful. This is just what the structure of the mass media forbids.

Indeed, the desert of standardization is encroaching on the few oases that have become established. As David Riesman has recently pointed out,* even those areas like jazz, which have provided adolescents with their traditional strongholds of individuality in taste and competence, are being thoroughly, if comparatively subtly, commercialized. There is less genuine individuality and variety in jazz, or hot-rodding, or photography, or anything else, as these activities develop their own house organs and require increasingly expensive equipment and intricate techniques. The *aficionado* is likely to find that he has fled from mass culture into an area of specialization in which he is no less subject to manipulation, and in which the prevailing norms are again effectively established by other persons for commercial purposes.

As more and more enclaves of autonomous activity are opened up commercially, the role of individual competence declines, to be replaced by discrimination in choice among mass-produced articles. The early hi-fi bugs built their own tuners and amplifiers from tubes,

* "Listening to Popular Music," *Individualism Reconsidered* (Glencoe, Ill.: The Free Press, 1954).

condensers, resistors, and so forth, individually selected according to their precise electrical properties. This is a hard job, requiring skills, like soldering, which are not directly related to electronics as such. So this stage did not last very long; most youngsters interested in hi-fi began to buy components instead; that is, completed tuners, amplifiers, and speakers, which could be combined as desired by simple electrical connection. This also required a fair understanding of electronics—nearly as much as before—for the right components must be selected to yield the effect desired with the money available; impedances must match, the equipment give its best performance in the frequency range the builder is interested in. But the manual skills and dexterities initially necessary to the hi-fi bug were no longer needed; hi-fi as a hobby became available then to a less specialized group of youngsters who had less in common.

The skill necessary even to select and assemble components, however, is far too great, and arouses too much insecurity, for people accustomed to going now and paying later; and they constitute a market too vast to be ignored. Our economy has come to rest largely on the money people do not have but expect to get. So hi-fi sets are now manufactured, delivered, and installed. The bug can still build his set for himself, if he wants to; he can still build a radio out of an oatmeal box and a crystal, if he wants to. But his isolation has been breached.

To the adolescent, this means that a resource which is conducive to autonomy is threatened. Hi-fi bugs, like other serious hobbyists, thrive on organized heterogeneity. The organizing principle is the competence they share; the disparate elements are contributed by their different personalities. When young people who are otherwise very different from one another share skills, goals, and a common area of experience, each helps the others to understand their own uniquenesses, which greatly facilitates self-definition. The common skills and goals provide a reference point; the differences then add dimensions. Building a hi-fi set with another boy who is just as good at it as you are, but richer, teaches you a lot about the difference in outlook between rich people and poorer ones.

But this does not happen if the organizing principle shrinks from shared competence to shared taste. If all it takes to join the hi-fi bugs is some terminology and some up-to-date information about what is considered best and what is not, there is no longer any fixed reference point and no perspective. All that can be learned is a thousandth variation on the art of being friendly with strangers. After that, you might as well go to the show and see Elvis again. It all comes to the same thing.

Adolescent growth is seriously blocked by anything that keeps youngsters from responding *specifically* to one another. Our cultural insistence on *generalized* patterns of response that ignore the significance of subtle but vital human differences is one of the things that most seriously impedes adolescence. Adults may find it annoying and tiresome to fritter themselves away in superficial intercourse with charming people whom they never see very clearly and who never really notice what they are like. But in adolescence this kind of empty socialization is not merely meaningless but dangerous. In the adolescent peer-group, youngsters not only teach one another; they learn one another. They learn to feel about others and about themselves, and in some cases to love. Respect for real competence—in the schoolroom, the shop, or the street; the football field or the living room; the driver's seat or the back seat of the car—respect for competence of mind, heart, and body is the trustworthy foundation on which love must be built.

I do not mean by this that people are loved for their skills; this, indeed, would be to treat man as a means rather than an end. But love must be realistic in the sense that it abjures magic and responds to the hard core of actuality in the person loved; it must be a response to the person-in-operation as a person, so to speak. Otherwise, it is not love but a sentimental fantasy aroused by manner or appearance, and often a form of illness as well.

The large, sensible insight behind coeducation is the understanding that it gives boys and girls opportunities to do things together. This discourages romance and favors love, which is a sound idea; for romance, like alcohol, should be enjoyed but must not be allowed to become necessary. But this often does not work, because the forces of triviality in modern life are stronger than those tending toward tenderness and understanding in individuals, so that what boys and girls actually get a chance to do together is not important enough to matter. Anyone could do it; the doing of it in no way expresses the unique qualities of the youngsters, who then never reveal themselves to each other. They never really experience each other as human beings.

Experience of and respect for the competence of other people establish their place in our scheme of things. It provides the connection between our feeling about them—whatever its quality—and our understanding of the processes with which we are involved. If this is essential to love, it is essential to much more as well, and much that is more immediately effective in making the world go round. Perception of others, widened by social sophistication and deepened by capacity for feeling, becomes *discriminating*. Variety in human relations, in response to real differences between what people are actually like and real differences in our relationship to them, becomes possible. We can feel; but we can also feel our way; we need depend on no formulae.

But the experience that young people have of others is influenced very strongly by factors other than their respective personalities. We can only experience other persons in a social context, and before we have had much experience of life we are usually unable to view our social context with any great detachment. It appears not only natural but inevitable; we cannot actually conceive of alternatives to it or of ourselves as having an existence independent of it.

We must therefore examine that social context rather closely, attending especially to the processes of self-definition. It is this social context that sets the conditions of tenderness and defines the kinds of competence that will be respected by adult society, in contrast to those—however adolescents may prize them—that it disparages.

Adolescents are affected by all social institutions. First, and most influential of all, is the family. The family, of course, is far more than a social instrument; it is not there just to deal with its children, care for them, and introduce them into adult society. As the home of its members the family has its own reason for being; it is an end in itself.

Then, there are the mass media—and in some profusion. Cartoonists may still depict the "teen-ager" lying on his back ensnarled in the telephone cord with a coke in one hand and a comic book in the other, as he does his scanty homework by the light of the television set; but adolescents have somewhat more varied tastes than this suggests. They watch, read, and listen to what everyone else does; and they also have special patterns of their own. The adolescent movie audience is now about all that is keeping the last few neighborhood cinemas from being turned into supermarkets; Hollywood now caters to what it believes to be their tastes and thereby keeps their tastes debased. There are journals like *Seventeen* and *Ivy Magazine* that are intended purely for adolescent readers and focused on the uniquely American adolescent market; for in this country, adults who deal with "teen-agers" must recognize that they have some money. Being patrons themselves, they cannot always be patronized.

Boys have the army to face, and this is a social institution indeed. Churches and communities have youth programs, which are useful precisely to the degree that they accept young people as they really are. If, instead, they set out to civilize the untamed, they are usually eluded; in this respect things have not changed much since Huck Finn fled from the Widow. Many adolescents have jobs, or are trying to find one; and some are in prison or reform school, which is an unambiguous social status. Some are fighting for sanity and health in hospitals.

But I believe I can show most clearly how social processes affect adolescent integrity by concentrating on *one* social institution. The chief formal social institution bearing on the adolescent is the high school—for some, the first years of college. The school is the official agent—the contemporary secular arm—by which society deals with adolescents. As such, the school is peculiarly representative of social forces and demands. It imposes these in a very different way from that of the mass media, the army, or the church. But it is haunted by the same *daemons* as the rest of our society.

The influence of our society on adolescence is not wholly benign. To focus attention on the school as the aggressive instrument of adolescent socialization is therefore in some measure to add to the burden of criticism to which the school has been rather continuously subjected for more than a decade. This of itself seems to me regrettable. The school has been attacked by experts, though usually by experts in something other than education, and seldom from the point of view that it is compromising its obligation to human growth and personality development. These are more frequently among the shibboleths of the school's defenders, who seem to me, on the whole, a more responsible group than its assailants.

Nevertheless, we are concerned with what happens to adolescents in American society. The school is where it usually happens, and where it is easiest to observe. The school is also morally responsible, in a way that social institutions that deal only incidentally with young people are not, for the welfare of youngsters as complete human beings. In the succeeding chapters I will try to analyze those aspects of the school's operation that affect adolescent self-definition most strongly. The task could be undertaken in many different ways, but most cogently, I believe, if I distinguish sharply between two fundamental dynamics: (1) self-definition through the clarification of experience; and (2) the establishment of self-esteem.

Chapter III

THE IMPACT OF THE SCHOOL:

The Clarification of Experience

In what ways does the school influence the growth of adolescents? It is society's formal provision for them. It is charged with their intellectual and moral development. In a culture like ours, in which tragedy is regarded as a problem and problems are assumed to have solutions, the school is held responsible for observable deficiencies in the adolescent much as a department store is held responsible for defects in the quality of its merchandise.

For the most part the school accepts this responsibility. It tries to meet it professionally; that is, by means of a program planned to meet stated objectives through techniques derived from empirical research. The statements of objectives are often so naïve philosophically, and derived from so vulgar a conception of what life will demand of its students, as to be indefensible; the research is often so stupidly planned and executed as to be irrelevant to the conclusions drawn from it. But the school is seldom frivolous or irresponsible in its attitude toward youngsters; it tries to understand its job and do it as conscientiously as the quality of its staff permits.

Indeed, in discussing the role of the school in the social order, professional educationists are frequently unrealistic through being *overly* responsible and conscientious in their point of view. They see the school as a much more active influence on society than it is. They may regard the school as primarily the agent of society, but they still perceive it as an *agent*. They assume that it can and does *act* rather independently, on behalf either of society or of its own educational ends, and that its policies, if properly executed, ought decisively to influence the outcome of events.

In this conception of the function of the school there is some truth; but the school overstates its agency. It takes too much on itself, and speaks as if it were responsible for the outcomes of social processes that it has scarcely influenced. For in much that transpires within the school—and that is undoubtedly highly educational—

the school is not an agent. It is the arena in which social forces interact, employing students, teachers, and administrative officials in roles with which they have become familiar but into which they have not developed much insight. The committee reports and public statements by which the school attests its professional orientation and benevolent concern are as sincerely meant as Polonius' advice to Laertes. But the school's intentions are seldom independent influences on educational events. The drama of Prince Hamlet did not work out quite as Polonius intended; and Polonius was not its hero. Too many other people were trying to do too many other things; and even the adolescent Hamlet, who came closest, did not quite grasp all that was going on.

What *is* going on? If we were to attempt to analyze the complex web of activity of a typical American high school with the affectionate but detached interest of an observer from another planet, what social functions would be discernible? They will obviously vary from one school to another and, more significantly perhaps, according to the categories of thought of the observer. But I think we might expect to find something like the following social processes occurring simultaneously and in interaction. I indicate them here in order of the importance I would attribute to their actual impact on the adolescent and on his subsequent life as an adult in society.

First: The school is where you learn to be an American. Americanization is a process, not a result; it is carried on chiefly by the youngsters themselves. The teachers play a fairly important role as manipulators of the *mise en scène;* but they do not much influence the process by direct instruction. There is plenty of nationalist propaganda in our textbooks and courses, but there is not much evidence that it influences the students. The informal processes of Americanization produce, in fact, so stubborn a resistance to direct indoctrination with any ideology that we have had to evolve other means of propagating our own. They are effective, and the school is one of the principal loci of their application; but they are informal and fit cleverly into our image of ourselves as an independent people given to irreverence.

Second: The school serves as a hydraulic mechanism designed to provide a measure of fluidity and stability of equilibrium for a society which is far more stratified than its members care to admit.

How a youngster reacts to the school largely determines his chance to get on in the world; whether he wants to get on in the world largely determines what his attitude toward the school will be. What the school contributes in the process is complex, and formal instruction is probably not a very important part of it. Those who set themselves professional goals receive some elementary instruction in the relevant sciences and techniques; it is not usually very good. For the rest, the vast majority, the school serves as what C. Wright Mills has called "a seed-bed of . . . white-collar skills." * For all, it is the source of the certification prerequisite to getting a decent job in a society grown much too impersonal to depend on face-to-face assessment of competence.

Third: The school transmits some of the knowledge and some of the intellectual skills and attitudes on which the tradition of Western civility depends—depends more precariously than ever. The quality of general education in the American high school is not high, particularly in comparison with a European secondary school of university preparatory grade. But it is probably underestimated by most observers. It has contributed substantially to the development of a middle class which is interested in the arts, capable of quite fine discrimination in consumption, intellectually alert and anxious to maintain a broad and just interest in its involvement in world affairs. This class continues, however, to lack sufficient depth of education and confidence in the authority of the mind to use its intellectual capacities fully.

Fourth: The school functions as an administrative and records center for various activities with reference to the young. The high school adds substantially to the dossier which has now become standard equipment for Americans. It records a youth's intelligence, interests, medical history, and emotional stability. It notes, should it occur, the rare complication produced by the development of political interests. It observes—and often sets down on microfilm, for permanence and economy—its appraisal of his personality and of his over-all promise for the future, and it transmits this appraisal, and sometimes the raw data on which the appraisal is based, in response to what it regards as legitimate inquiry, forever afterward.

* In an unpublished address before the New Orleans Conference of the Center for the Study of Liberal Education for Adults, 3 April, 1954.

It is probably idle to question at this point whether these processes are conducive to the good of society; they are in any event part of its workings. Processes having a similar function have always occurred in schools. One can hardly imagine a school system which did not somehow provide an ambience congenial to the values and attitudes of the culture which supported it. In every society complex enough to provide formal schooling for postpubescent youngsters, the schools strongly influence the social mobility of individuals. In every culture education aims to develop individuals whose sensitivities and whose anxieties will be useful and reassuring to the kind of people who already wield power. (Indeed, the distinction between liberal and professional education seems to be peculiar to an age of self-made men. Harvard College was founded as a vocational school for clergymen; it was hardly necessary to stipulate that it should also turn out Harvard men.) And schools have doubtless always managed to provide interested authorities with estimates of their students' character and potential for various kinds of action; in this, as today, their judgments were colored by the ideologies then prevailing.

These functions are traditional, but their impact upon the adolescent is new. They become something different in a society in which school attendance is universal and compulsory, the educational establishment correspondingly enormous, the teaching staff correspondingly specialized, bureaucratic, and lacking in prestige and self-esteem.

Regardless of the uses to which any society may put its schools, education has an obligation that transcends its own social function and society's purposes. That obligation is to clarify for its students the meaning of their experience of life in their society. The school exists fundamentally to provide the young people of a community —a nation may be a community; it had better be—with a fairly tough and firmly fixed philosophical apparatus for making a certain kind of sense out of their lives, and communicating with other people who may be assumed to have a basically similar apparatus.

This does *not* mean propagating similar views, or social attitudes and beliefs as such. A great deal of this sort of propagandizing does go on concomitantly and perhaps inevitably, but it is not helpful in accomplishing the purpose of clarification. Neither does it mean teaching the truth—though it certainly does mean not teaching the false—for the truth usually cannot be taught; it is too subtle and iridescent, and can only be recognized by persons who expect that it will look entirely different when viewed from different angles. The first and fundamental step is certainly to get the relevant facts right, if facts are involved, and deal with them honestly and consistently; facts can be taught. But they are not the truth.

What it does mean is teaching people to mean the same thing by the truth; to establish in their minds similar categories of thought; to approach understanding with roughly the same unconscious predispositions; to admit the same considerations as relevant; to share a common intellectual—though it sometimes is scarcely that—methodology. In any generation, a few souls will use this apparatus to formulate the truth about themselves and the world they live in; and they do not necessarily go mad or get themselves hanged. We simply remember more vividly those who do. But the social purpose of education is not to create a nation of actively insatiable truth-seekers; truth-seeking is a highly specialized function. It is to create a nation which can see clearly, and agree on what it sees, when it looks in certain directions.

The American school seems to do this. We do indeed share a common culture. There is as yet no other nation in which individual regional differences have been so swamped. Whether the man from the car rental agency meets you at New York, Miami, New Orleans, or San Francisco International Airport hardly matters. And the commonness goes further: American mass gratifications, from soft drinks to comic books and movies, have turned out to be the common coin of mass culture the world over; so that it hardly matters either whether he meets you in Ankara, Tokyo, or Rome. This is not conquest, but genuine cultural diffusion. All over the world, man in the mass has turned out to be exactly our type of fellow.

It is nearly as deep as it is wide, too. As we view ourselves being ourselves, the differences between the patterns of lives of city folk and country folk, rich people and poor ones, those with a Ph.D. and those who never finished grade school are minimal. There are, of course, superficial differences in *how* and *where* people of different social groups spend their leisure, but not fundamental differences in what they *do* with it and what it does to them.

Our schools are a precise expression of our culture; they do prevent it flying apart; they do polarize our vision in certain directions; they do certainly establish in young Americans common categories of thought and unconscious predispositions. But they do not clarify the meaning of experience.

Our schools act as if America were still a melting pot. This is a strong tradition that developed through the decades when the nation was being built up through immigration. Free public secondary education was created in the United States in order to supply its expanding economy with a labor force and a technical staff equal to its growing demands. In order to do so, it had to take youngsters from the most diverse ethnic backgrounds and turn them into an article sufficiently standardized to fit efficiently into a productive system that had very little interest in their personal characteristics and no wish to be troubled by them. In return, the youngsters could count on a rising standard of living. The high school was intended to produce not an industrial proletariat, but a group of individuals who could be trusted with complex technical and administrative machinery and trusted not to raise awkward questions about the place of that machinery in the universe of values. The youngsters by and large agreed with the high school that they were being given an unprecedented opportunity.

Still, adolescents need clarity. If adolescence is the process of defining oneself through conflict with society, it is helpful if the educational institutions with which the adolescent must deal remain loyal throughout the struggle to the task of clarifying the meaning of experience. For him this amounts, after all, to the same thing: one defines oneself by clarifying the meaning of one's experience. As an individual, he is responsible for achieving more clarity than the school can give him; for the school's cultural biases will in any case camouflage many vitally important phenomena and relationships. Each youngster must correct as best he can for the astigmatism induced by social institutions. But if the school is consistent, honest, and sufficiently sophisticated to be aware of important things and coherent about the relations between them, it will be of great assistance in giving the adolescent something on which to build himself.

Adolescents are ill-served by schools which act as melting pots. When they get into a stew, it is best if the stew is like a properly prepared Japanese soup: crystal clear, with the individual qualities of all the odd ingredients preserved; the soft things soft, the tough things tough, the green things green, and the yellow things yellow. From this kind of heterogeneity it is possible to learn something.

In this respect, the high school has been getting worse for years, for society has. It has always devoted itself to the interests of uniformity more than to individuality; but the uniformities used to be more *external* than they are now. I shall not labor this point, which has already been dealt with so thoroughly by Riesman, W. L. Whyte, and many others; but will simply point out that the school today is less a stew pot than a blender. What comes out, when it is functioning effectively, is not merely uniform but bland and creamy; by its very nature inimical to clarity, yet retaining in a form difficult to detect all the hostile or toxic ingredients present in the original mixture.

This is really serious. It is one thing for the schools of a culture to impart to adolescents a distorted picture of reality, seen from a limited point of view, but *clearly*. So long as the school is not simply an agent of propaganda, or psychotic—so long, that is, as what it talks about is really there, even if what it says is much different from the whole truth—it may still contribute effectively to adolescent growth. Adolescents are alive, and the school is not the whole of life; given a consistent, honest, and coherent picture of the world, they can correct for themselves its biases and omissions. But it is quite another thing for the school to limit perception and responsiveness in every direction to what the society can tolerate without discord. Society thereby establishes within its members a cut-off point; no matter what happens, they do not see too much, get too involved, or try to overthrow the system.

This is happening increasingly in our schools; though nobody intends that it should—in principle, that is; the school staff do intend that it should in particular instances. When a specific conflict arises, the school almost automatically seeks to *mediate* rather than to clarify. It assesses the power of the conflicting interests, works out a compromise among them, and keeps its name out of the papers. The loyalty oath is accepted with gentle chidings about singling out teachers for undue suspicion; *The Merchant of Venice* is omitted from the reading list in favor of something just as good in which all the Jewish characters are pleasant; the aggressive candidate for student council member is quietly barred from office on grounds of emotional immaturity.

We do not know that universal education can retain a commitment to clarity; being in the business, I am sometimes skeptical of it myself. The problem is one of dignity. We have had in all history no experience of any society in which a large proportion of the members could take a good, hard look at life without breaking and running. The examined life has always been pretty well confined to a privileged class. Liberal thought has held that this confinement was deliberate: the members of the privileged class knew that knowledge was power, and excluded those subordinate to them so as to maintain the existing inequities. Liberal thought was here based on sound observation. But is was inclined to overlook certain converse processes.

The most important privilege of a privileged class is freedom from some of the vicissitudes of fortune. Its members are running the show and can divert much that is disagreeable elsewhere. It is often easier, therefore, for them to be honest with themselves about what they see and about what it portends. They can afford to be; they have to be if they are not to lose control, and control is important to them. Ruling classes differ, of course, in the degree to which they understand this and can bear to go on understanding it. De Tocqueville, standing at the point of no return in history, noticed that the *ancien régime français* had forgotten it, and that we had not learned it. Most elites do forget it, and become convinced that destiny, rather than equestrian skill, is keeping them in the saddle. Their members can be distinguished in historical engravings by the hoofprints in the small of their backs.

With respect to this issue, our expectations of education are mixed and conflicting. Our public-school system was not designed to nurture an elite—just the contrary; it was designed to train the boys who would work uncomplainingly in its mills and vote unquestioningly for its measures. The school, by and large, is still devoted to the twin ideals of success and contentment, though it pursues them with greater technical sophistication. But our cultural tradition is a lot broader than our school system, and is less purely pragmatic. It is slightly Hellenistic, a good deal more British, and in any case humanistic and Western. Whether we want to or not, when we think of education—rather than of what school was really like—we think of a process which is expected to prepare the young to accede as well as to succeed. Educators like Robert Hutchins have maintained that democracy demands just this view of public education because in it every man must behave as a ruler of men.

This seems to me rather fanciful, because what actually happens in a modern democratic state seems to be abdication of popular sovereignty in favor of an equally undistinguished and ephemeral ruling clique. But this does not erase the connection, established in our minds by a hardy tradition of our culture, between education and a large measure of responsibility, detachment, and discipline.

In this tradition the common man, exposed as he is to economic, social, and personal pressures, has never fully shared. That, given the opportunity, he would consent to do so is merely an educated guess. He has not yet received the protections of status and property on which the tradition was based; these, or their equivalent, are only now being devised in the form of a less completely material conception of the welfare state in which new social forms guarantee leisure and continued high-level economic security rather than bare survival.

New and more widely applicable sources of security and status also lead to a clearer sense of self. *Lucky Jim* is just as trustworthy and really just as brave as Archdeacon Grantly, as well as a great deal more human. But he is far less sure of himself; he cannot count on his nerves and judgment as well in a threatening situation, and situations have much more power to threaten him. He is more vulnerable; he has a much shorter lease on life.

The modern school, then, serves people who lack the protections enjoyed by those who taught us what to expect of an educated class. It is also staffed by people who are, in fact, vulnerable to public opinion and dependent on the approval and support of their colleagues, even in matters of detail, in order to be effective. We cannot be sure that they will ever feel free themselves, or accept any large measure of responsibility to teach youngsters to examine what they are learning against the criteria of their own values, traditions, and experience of life. It may be that we cannot expect them to analyze experience sharply, and tell the truth about what the analysis reveals.

It is difficult to put what we feel to be wrong into words, and we very often use the wrong ones. We complain that standards are too low; yet research report after research report confirms that students, by and large, are learning more rather than less of the kind of fact and simple skill on which schools conventionally base their claim. We feel that the students are getting lazier; but they seem to work hard, and the worst of all often work the hardest of all; they voluntarily assail the teacher with volumes of mediocrity because, they say, they want to raise their grade. Students who do badly in a course frequently argue that they should have a higher mark because what they did took them so long. We feel the students are duller, and it is true that the public school reaches students of lower ability than it was formerly able to enroll. But it is not they who are the focus of public concern; in fact it is precisely with them that the school often does its most clearly professional and original work. We feel that the students are less disciplined, and are here a little closer to the mark. But it is an inner discipline that is lacking; the school fails to provide a basis for it. The undisciplined behavior which sometimes results is often a sign of the anguish which results from having no core of one's own.

Standards are unsatisfactory, not because they are low, but because they are fragmentary and incoherent. They exist, and to the extent that they exist, they add to the general confusion. The academic curriculum consists of shards of a pre-democratic academic culture; relics of a way of life in which many of the people who had gone through school read poetry for fun, spelled properly and wrote cogently because they sometimes worked on public documents, spoke French correctly and fluently because they occasionally had to communicate as equals with civilized Frenchmen. Their schools were technically far worse than ours; the teachers untrained in the special concerns of education, usually unimaginative and occasionally brutal. But in that culture, as in ours, the students were quick to learn what made sense in relation to their view of themselves and their social role, either with the school's help or despite it.

The problem today is to determine what does make sense in terms of one's view of oneself and one's social role. Our schools are socially heterogeneous, and deeply riven by discontinuities of experience between the staff, the students, and those earlier individuals who wrote the major works and participated in the events with which the curriculum must deal. Between the high-school staff and the street corner boy there is no common ground. Between the high-school staff and Shakespere there is not likely to be much common ground either. If Sir John Falstaff can only reach the corner boy— who would find him very meaningful—by passing through the high school, he is pretty sure to get lost on the way.

This social heterogeneity is not simply a matter of incongruous courses of study and students with very diverse cultural backgrounds. These would be, as they are commonly thought to be, unique strengths of our system, if only the school had a philosophical structure by which to order them—not into a hierarchy, but according to the existing and potential relationships among them and a coherent set of values. A school having white and Negro students ought to be able, for example—if it is sustained by a conception of democracy that is both profound and sophisticated—to make use of the problems attending desegregation as a living exercise in American social democracy as it actually is. This would require intense historical scholarship and keen and detached sociological analysis. But neither the teachers nor the students are usually capable of either; faced with so controversial an issue they would more likely panic when they found that they lacked the necessary scholarly skills and discipline, and each would run to his particular pressure group to try to get his story in first.

The social changes of the past century have been diastrophic in magnitude; they have produced faulting in several different planes. Growth and education, which depend on continuity of meaning, are likely to be suddenly arrested by running into social groups or institutions—within the school as well as outside it—which are *intrusive* in every sense of the word and which, developmentally speaking, ought not to be there at all. Parents intercede directly with the principal or even the school board to get their children grades high enough to admit them to an Ivy League college. The janitor becomes a channel for gossip that originates among the he-men of the vocational departments as they play poker in the boiler room.* Neighbors, peeping through the lace curtains of their parlors, complain

* Wilbur B. Brookover, *A Sociology of Education* (New York: American Book Co., 1955), pp. 196-202.

that students are walking to school in Bermuda shorts just as if they came from rich homes. Student publications are scanned by committees of self-styled mothers, and textbooks and syllabi by committees of self-appointed patriots, for signs of heterodoxy. Teachers who pride themselves on their toughness indignantly whisper that young Mr. So-and-So who cannot keep order in class ought not to be given tenure; and that the principal, if he ever fails to support them after they have mishandled a problem of discipline, does not know how to run a school. Nobody is ever told not to interfere in matters he does not understand.

This lack of philosophical structure I should judge to be the chief obstacle to the development of high-school curricula which would use our best cultural resources to help students make sense out of the lives they actually lead. The resources are there. One really has to be either a cultural snob or a professional alarmist to feel that American arts are barren today. Our poetry is good; our ballet may well be the best in the world; we have excellent literary critics, and they have excellent critics of their own; the *Partisan Review* snaps at the *New Yorker* with the colorful fury of a moray eel attacking a parrotfish. The novel is said to be dying, and it is perhaps a clumsy form in which to attack the existential problems of contemporary life; but it is also extremely broad in scope. Every social level, every sort of human and administrative relationship now receives serious treatment in respectable literary work. The social sciences are not so flourishing; work expressing the seminal ideas of a reflective and experienced specialist has yielded prominence to the teamwork of well-financed committees. But this is comprehensive and disciplined enough to yield insights useful to adolescents, even if not very original or individualized. The natural sciences seem to have abdicated the responsibility for commenting on the meaning of human existence, which they discharged enthusiastically through Einstein's lifetime, and this is a real loss, for only science can hope to keep technology in some sort of moral order. Still, there is quite a lot to work with.

American artists and intellectuals are addressing themselves competently to a very wide range of issues deeply relevant to modern life. But the schools no longer accept intellectual and humanistic authority. The prestige of the intellectual and artist in America is not as low as intellectuals and artists feel; in fact, it is quite high. Nevertheless, they are merely one of the heterogeneous components of American social life. Most school personnel would probably agree, if the statement were made to them, that the function of the humanities is to illuminate life. But they have not grown up with any personal experience of using the humanities for this purpose; and they enthusiastically or apathetically mishandle them. They fear that students will find passages too difficult, and assume that it is the artist's job to say no more than can be easily understood. They fear that the American Legion or a Catholic action group will object to the implications of other passages, and they also fear that they themselves will be called censors; so rather than suppress a work, they set up committees to *edit* it and forestall any possible objections. They note details which they regard as errors from the viewpoint of their own special interests and pounce upon them; if the administration clears Ibsen's *Ghosts* with the PTA by warning it that *Ghosts* is a classic and can therefore be allowed to deal with venereal disease, the chairman of the biology department will be noisily unhappy because it deals with venereal disease inaccurately.

The staff and the students may approve of the use of materials which, if properly handled, would clarify the meaning of modern experience. They approve of most advances. But their total experience of life has not fitted them to use the best of these materials with respect for their properties. They are like a housewife who enjoys hearing about what the science of nutrition can do for her family, but who has no interest in learning what vitamins are destroyed by heat and which minerals are washed out by boiling. It is up to God and Birdseye to put these things in so they will survive any short cuts she may take.

Unlike the housewife, the school is apt to accept considerable responsibility for the solution of technical and methodological problems. But it cannot apply this sense of technical responsibility to the problem of maintaining meanings in its curriculum. It has no sense of texture or structure with reference to meanings, and is likely to be antagonized by any difficulties it encounters, recognizing in them a residual implication of social inferiority. The school may get as far as translating the problem of meaning into the problem of communication; that is, the problem of determining what may be said or done in the school that can be understood by a maximum number of very different students with a minimum of effort. It is not likely to get much further, or to have a sympathetic understanding of how its quest for simplicity rather than meaning reduces its power to clarify the lives of students.

It is easy to mistake the urgent technical difficulties of teaching a heterogeneous student group for the moral and developmental problems, less urgent and far more serious, which it creates; it is easy to solve the former expediently and evade the latter. Some of the youngsters, for example, are juvenile delinquents or are growing up in slums; they may have become a threat to the manners and morals of more decorous middle-class boys and girls. Some of them have begun thinking and reading in the classroom, and are making the others feel inferior. A teacher, threatened with a switchblade knife, fears at the very least a certain loss of face. Undoubtedly, something must be done about it.

But just what must be done ought to be determined by the school's perception of its function. The problem of preventing a boy from slashing up a teacher is not so simple morally. A juvenile delinquent and a middle-class teacher are incompatible; yet the school is supposed to be able to guide itself by its own purposes, and the human relationship between boy and teacher is its most powerful instrument for achieving its purposes. If the main purpose of the school is to clarify the meaning of experience, its response must do a good deal more than protect the teacher. It must convey to the boy the school's determination to maintain order in its own house; its respect for boys as human beings; its anger at him for having abused that respect in this instance; and its sense of the provocation to which slum boys are sometimes subjected by middle-class behavior. It must convey to the teacher confidence that he will be supported in his role and an awareness that he has probably been playing it badly. It must get the boy and the teacher working together again on the development of the boy as a human being.

The school may do it, too; it will certainly try, and this is greatly to its credit. The American school system has come to conceive itself, in principle and on a very wide scale, as something more than a law-enforcement agency when confronted with student behavior that it cannot accept. The school is now likely to see youngsters who break its regulations as the victims of a maladjustment in the relationship between it and themselves, rather than as miscreants to be punished. It very often applies this point of view sentimentally and has been subjected to a great deal of derision for adopting it. It frequently fails to live up to this view in practice, because in practice the school usually assumes that it is the *youngster*, rather than the relationship or the school itself, that needs to be readjusted. But the viewpoint must, in my judgment, be accepted as one of the few major advances in decency that the twentieth century can justly claim.

The difficulty is that the school seldom goes about applying it with enough dignity and self-confidence to help the student in defining himself. Its motives are weighted toward administrative expedience rather than toward awareness of what is going on in the youngster and respect for what he is and what he may become, even though these more humane motives are now stronger than in the past. Where a full human response to him would previously have been blocked by arrogance, rigidity, and punitiveness, it is now blocked by status anxiety, manipulativeness, and the absence of a firm habit of respect for individuality of any kind. The school has lost confidence in its authority to maintain order, and has specially trained experts to crawl inside the miscreant, exorcise him from himself, and engineer his consent to its guidance. But even a boy who pulls a knife on a teacher—the action is actually rather rare—is entitled to respect for his privacy and some security against invasion. He may need counseling; he may need a formal and effective paddling; he may need a little money and a decent job; he may need glasses and a longer knife. But he does not need to be treated as a problem in social integration. Nobody does.

Yet the school attacks the problems of self-definition in a heterogeneous student group as if they were problems in social integration. Integration is the only attack a school that works like a blender can take; no matter how hard it tries, the problem of preserving the integrity of individual experience is beyond it.

This is the approach to morality that grows out of our cultural situation. The most important social process taking place in the high school is learning to be an American. But so much of learning to be an American is learning not to let your individuality become a nuisance. We conceive our country as having achieved a position of leadership and dominance by carefully subordinating personal and ethnic disparity to the interests of teamwork in a colossal technical and administrative enterprise. For us, conformity is a moral mandate. When we insist on taking a personal stand and bucking the system, we feel not only anxious, but guilty as well.

Much as the American tendency to conformity has been emphasized recently, this point, it seems to me, has been understressed. We do conform, but not primarily (as is supposed) because of fear and alienation. There is a strong positive element in our conformity; we do not merely huddle together in little smug or frightened clusters. One has only to watch a committee at work to see that consensus is regarded as a good thing in itself, and intransigence a bad one. The members are eager to accept one another's point of view; awkward data are dismissed, not cynically, but as an act of public spirit. The old joke about a statesman needing the ability to rise above principle turns out to be no joke; an individual who cannot is made to feel as willfully self-indulgent as a timid courtesan in an old, established house.

We are an obsessively moral people, but our morality is a team morality. What is good for the team is good for the player; fair play means playing according to the rules and asking for* no special advantage. It is important to win, but the passions of victory must not lead to personal pride, the passions of defeat to personal anger or permanent resentment.

On the team, individual differences must be minimized. "Who cares about his race, religion, or national origin—he can pitch!" baseball players constantly exhort one another; so, at least, the posters of the Mayor's Council Against Discrimination proclaim. Yet, discrimination seems an odd thing to be against. One would like to suppose that Jews and Negroes are now admitted to the local chapters of an increasing number of college fraternities because these have finally adopted a policy of *greater* discrimination rather than less, and are basing their discrimination on factors of greater im-

---

* Cf. Chapter 8, "Reflections on the American Identity," of Erik Homburger Erikson's *Childhood and Society* (New York: Norton, 1950) for a most insightful exposition of this point.

mediate relevance to what a boy could contribute to fraternity life —possibly through the very differences in character and personality that stem from his unusual race, religion, or national origin. This, in fact, is probably what *is* happening, but we dislike putting it so, even though confidence that differences enrich is a basic article of liberal faith. It is no article of American faith. We know what "discrimination" means in our language, and it does not mean sensitivity to significant differences.

Or perhaps it does, and this is what we are against. Our melting pot really works, and even the most stupid and vicious of us is beginning to believe that race no longer refers to any meaningful heritage, that Jews share nothing significant in Judaism. This is integration with a vengeance, and a victory for democracy to delight the heart of the bitterest anti-Semite. The exotic toxins have been almost all absorbed, denatured, removed from the robust bloodstream of American life. America's rugged institutions have been too much for them altogether. They are lost, assimilated; and no organ of society has done so much to assimilate them as the school system.

The process of becoming an American, as it goes on in high school, tends to be a process of renunciation of differences. This conflicts directly, of course, with the adolescent need for self-definition; but the conflict is so masked in institutionalized gaiety that the adolescent himself usually does not become aware of it. He must still deal with the alienation it engenders. He may do this by marginal differentiation, like Riesman's glad-handing boy with the special greeting style.* He may do it by erupting into bouts of occasionally violent silliness, which does not make him seem queer to other people because it is unconsciously recognized as a form of self-abnegation rather than self-assertion, and is not, therefore, threatening. He may, if he has sufficient ego-strength, become the adolescent equivalent of a genuine revolutionary—rather than a rebel—that is, he may actually succeed in rejecting the folkways of the school without identifying with them and becoming guilty and raucous; he can then replace them with constructive patterns of behavior

* David Riesman, in collaboration with Reuel Denney and Nathan Glazer, *The Lonely Crowd* (New Haven: Yale University Press, 1950), p. 82.

based on his own homemade values. This is a position which may lead to the growth of a splendid human being, but one which imposes a considerable strain on the boy.

In any case, he is unlikely to get much help from the school's routines. The constant attention to his adjustment; the ratings on cooperativeness and citizenship; the informal but virtually universal policy of limiting the number of failing grades in each class, which undercuts the meaning of competence in the classroom; the mock democratic institutions for student government and student discipline with their committees, juries, and rather studied use of informality to weaken any possible effort he might make to stand on his rights—all these work against him. On his side he has a variable number of factors: possibly a residual academic tradition in certain teachers that leads them to respect his competence; possibly a real evolving political competence of his own that makes him something of an adolescent statesman; possibly a family which is not sympathetic to "groupsy" values; possibly himself. Some youngsters resist standardization very well.

So much for Americanization. The other three social functions of the school also play very important parts in the clarification of experience. The next I mentioned, in order of importance, was the school's role in the distribution of status: in teaching students that they ought to want to get ahead in the world, how to go about doing it, what the terms are on which it can be done. Obviously, the process involves many value-assumptions and conscious and unconscious responses to subtle social cues; it therefore bears on the meaning of experience very fundamentally. However, this process is directly relevant to another aspect of adolescent growth—the establishment of a basis for self-esteem—which I shall treat in the next chapter. We shall look at this function more closely then.

I have already briefly considered certain relationships of the next of these social processes to the clarification of experience. This is the function we commonly mean by education: formal instruction in the natural and social sciences and the humanities—the impact of the school's course of study itself. I have said that this works rather better than it usually gets credit for, and that the most difficult obstruction to the school's use of major cultural resources for the clarification of experience is that the school is now so socially heterogeneous. A large proportion of the students and staff come from social groups in which the authority of the mind and its work is simply not accepted. From the arts they expect diversion and decoration; from the sciences the solution to technical problems; they demand these quickly and under all conditions without back talk. They have had no experience of the arts and sciences as elucidators of life, and mishandle and emasculate them in such a way that their power to serve is impaired or destroyed. Even though the arts now address themselves with profound respect and reduced sentimentality to the experiences of the common life, and the sciences consider its dynamics in detail, the school still regards them in practice as essentially external devices and adornments.

We are, of course, a sufficiently barbarous people to delight in both devices and adornments, so the curriculum includes an enormous lot of good things and handles them with a commendable if superficial sophistication. I suspect it will be a long time before an American high-school drama club performs *Aaron Slick of Punkin Crick* again. *No Exit* is in every way superior; it takes only four actors and one set, and Sartre has *cachet*. The youngsters and the school, in fact, enjoy the complex moral message of the play. It teaches us that in death as in life people who want to get along must cooperate; it teaches us that Hell is like a bad hotel; heaven, by contrast, is probably very much like the Caribe Hilton, with lots of charming, well-to-do people around the pool. Sartre shows keen insight into the moral problems of our day; and the school by producing him shows its courageous determination to grapple with them.

There are listening rooms and good record collections from which a high-school student can learn to appreciate music and consume it intelligently. There is the band, which doubles in brass as a social organization, lends color to athletic spectacles, keeps in time to the drum majorettes, and teaches everybody the value of teamwork. It appears in public, and it sounds good. There are classes in painting and sculpture with excellent Kodachrome slides of classical and contemporary masterpieces; in their own work, the school encourages the students to be creative, which means at least undisciplined but sometimes something more.

Students participate in seminars on all kinds of current social and scientific problems, sometimes carried on the local TV. These ought surely to lead to clarity and understanding, for rigorous precautions are taken. Books on the subject are discussed in class prior to the seminar; not usually the books with most to say, but those most suited to the student's level of reading comprehension. The organizers of the seminar are careful to see that everyone participates, and that all possible points of view are given equal time. There is a mediator, whose function is to continually focus the discussion, which means to demonstrate that the participants are not in fundamental disagreement; and to summarize the main points that have emerged, thus demonstrating that progress has been made toward more agreement. There is usually even a resource person who has been selected because he knows something about the topic and cautioned to keep his comments neutral and factual so that no biases will be introduced. There is no actual rehearsal, which would not be fair; but none is needed since the procedure is similar in practice and identical in its underlying assumptions to the daily procedures of the classroom.

In this way, the very concept of intellectual authority derived from competence and insight is prevented from ever becoming established. No educated person, recalling those steps in his education of which he was conscious, would hit on anything remotely like this. Schools may never have done much to further clarity of mind, though they have seldom in the past systematically sought to derive authority by pooling the viewpoints of persons incompetent to testify on the questions at issue. But the schools cannot forestall clarity altogether. All education is ultimately self-education, and it occurs even under quite adverse circumstances. Clear-minded adolescents do emerge, not unwillingly, from the American high school.

The last social function I attributed to the school—and, to an even greater degree, the college—was that of serving as an administrative center in which a dossier is compiled on each student's health, character, personality, and predilection for social action. This, since it is done as inconspicuously as possible and often by utter stealth, might seem to have little influence on the school's contribution to the clarification of the adolescent's experience. Actually it has an enormous—often a decisive—effect.

The school uses its student records as a basis for dealing with individuals and agencies outside the school. What goes into them determines, of course, the school's recommendations to prospective employers and the answers it gives to security agents. The information that it gives about what it regards as maturity or emotional stability, or about the student's political attitudes if he dared to develop any, can set his career back for a decade. Students—perhaps fortunately—are well aware of this and correspondingly cautious and skeptical about making use of the school's services. I have seldom heard, except at a performance of *Faust,* laughter as sardonic as that with which a student assembly greeted a recent statement by an apologist for their school's guidance service that "Security agents are *not* permitted access to our files—only to a summary of the relevant material in them." The statement, incidentally, was quite true, though not quite reassuring.

Schools, too, are aware that this is a problem, and "Confidentiality of student records" is frequently on the agenda of personnel groups.* But their discussions tend to center on externals: on whether the school can maintain viable public relations if it gets a reputation for not cooperating with the FBI or its local equivalent; whether students are being frightened away altogether and reducing the case load on which budgets ultimately depend; or, more piously, on just where the moral responsibility of the school lies in a conflict of interest between student and society.

I am much more worried about the effect on the student's inner life and emotional dynamics. By permitting agencies outside the student-counselor relationship to use its records, the school strikes at the very roots of clarity and growth. It invades the unconscious and disrupts the processes by which meanings are organized there by throwing up barriers of anxiety against self-understanding. That it has made it dangerous for the student to deal honestly with it is shameful, but not frightening; that it has made it dangerous for the student to deal honestly with himself is alarming; for to make unconscious processes dangerous is to forestall them. For example, a courageous boy who has come to feel that he has been drinking too much

* Cf. "Students Wary of Psychiatrists," a special report by Emma M. Harrison to *The New York Times* of October 24, 1956, of an address by Dr. Orville Rogers, former director of the Yale University Department of University Health to the annual Mental Health Forum of New York State.

—and needs help badly—may be able by conscious effort to force himself to go to the therapist, even though he knows that this may stain his record; he is a person, and he makes a choice. But if one major factor in his excessive drinking is repressed homosexual longing—as in our culture, among young men, it often is—he probably will not be able to get the help he needs, because his perfectly realistic anxiety about revealing this to the school will keep him from becoming conscious of it himself and making it accessible to therapy.

This is tragic. Many schools have interrupted the development of one of their most valuable and rapidly developing areas of service to students in order to set themselves up as Little Brother and Junior G-Man. The incidence of serious emotional disturbance in American life is high, and it is high among adolescents. The old name for schizophrenia, after all, was *dementia praecox,* which referred to the frequency with which gross symptoms of alienation tended to appear precociously—in adolescence rather than at a later age. This is evidence not that adolescents are emotionally unstable, but that in adolescence a human being is crucially devoted to building a stable and consistent self, and that any latent difficulties are likely to show themselves dramatically.

The anxieties of modern life have certainly not made adolescence any easier, and a large proportion of individual boys and girls do need professional help with problems of emotional development. The school is the logical place to give such help, if it can be arranged; it involves least disruption of the youngster's routine of life and least dramatization of his plight, which not only saves him pain and embarrassment but keeps the therapeutic process more effectively tied, as it should be, to the daily realities of living.

There has not been very much the school could do until recently, because there were no psychotherapeutic procedures that could safely be undertaken by nonmedical personnel, or that in any case were not so protracted, costly, and completely individualized as to be unfeasible for more than a handful of students. But this is no longer true. Individual psychoanalysis is still the therapy most clinicians would recommend for a very sick youngster, and it is still unavailable to most. But there have been two developments which have proved most helpful in the school situation, which require neither medically trained personnel nor a protracted series of individual sessions. These are the client-centered psychotherapy, developed by Carl Rogers and his associates over the past decade, which is designed to give considerable help in relatively few sessions; and various techniques of group psychotherapy, client-centered and other, which permit a skilled clinician to help a reasonable number of quite disturbed individuals—say, ten—at the same time, and to help them to help one another.

Client-centered and group psychotherapists must be carefully trained professional people; but they need not be physicians, and it is customary for them to accept appointments to the staffs of schools, school systems, or educational clinics. But their services to students are as fully dependent as those of a psychoanalyst on mutual trust between therapist and client and on unconscious processes. The unconscious processes in therapy are themselves dependent on this trust. There is no question of will involved; if the client fears or distrusts the therapist—quite a different matter from disliking him —fruitful associations and insights simply do not occur. Whatever we may, as good Freudians, think of our Censor, we must agree that it tries to protect us when it can; that is what it is for.

It is therefore usually impossible for a disturbed adolescent to accept any help, even if he is willing to risk it, from a therapist who may be building up a dossier against him. The session must be con‑ fidential; the student must be certain that his material will be used by others, at most, purely for research and in disguised form. School principals and deans who permit their personnel records to be used for administrative or security purposes find that they are no longer really offering a therapeutic service of which students can effectively avail themselves, even though they wish to regard this as still their major function.

Then, those students to whom the clarification of experience has become a mortal necessity are beyond the help of the school, cut off by the school's choice to add yet one more to its diverse group of public functions. To argue that the school is obligated to provide the agencies of legitimate government with personal information about its students because it is itself a public agency seems to me vicious nonsense. The school has indeed an obligation to society: to provide all the resources it can in support of the necessary intellec‑

tual and moral growth of future citizens. The record of the American school in this respect has been most seriously marred by the frequency with which it has willingly set its responsibility aside in order to perform a minor chore for the community or for influential private groups, from the maintenance of athletic spectacles to blood drives. But it might at least have drawn the line at serving as a police spy.

Perhaps the political realities seldom permit the school to maintain the privacy of its students against local vigilance or governmental agents of inquiry. But one cannot have much familiarity with American public education and retain the belief that this is the fundamental reason why the school so often does not maintain it. There is seldom much desire to, much conviction that it ought to be maintained. What is most seriously lacking is not merely courage but dignity. There is no sense of one's own business and the propriety of minding it; no professional pride in the legitimate restriction of the school's function to its own professional responsibilities such as any physician must have if he is to walk through a patient's home without reading the mail on his desk.

All schools appraise their students; if the appraisal deals with competence and character, which are the school's legitimate responsibility, it is obligated to do so. The high school must obviously inform the college candidly of its judgment of an applicant's chances for a successful college career, whether or not this blasts his hopes of admission; otherwise the college cannot accurately select students who can profitably use its services. It must give prospective employers a candid judgment as to whether a student can be trusted to do a job well. It is true that personality is now demonstrably a more important influence on subsequent success than competence, and that we must now live in an ideologically divided world. It may be argued, then, that the school is merely being realistic in including personality, social, and political attitudes in its appraisal. Have not these greater bearing on the decisions that must be made about the student than his mathematical aptitude, grade-point average, or his ability to perform work undertaken consistently and responsibly?

No doubt. But it is precisely the need to live in a world in which one is judged more by personality than by character, more by flexibility than competence, that fragments adolescent experience and injures the growing boy or girl. The dossier-building school contributes to their difficulties and betrays its primary responsibility to the growth of students as human beings free to feel and think as deeply as their experience of life permits, with no more anxiety or constraint than can be avoided.

The record of the school as a contributor to the clarification of the meaning of the adolescent life is, in the balance, poor. Its specific consequences seem to me usually negative. Good is done, too; but almost because things are not working quite right. The system falters: and scholarly teachers, warmly understanding and professionally oriented counselors, appear and sustain themselves on the satisfactions of their work till their colleagues catch them at it. Pockets of privacy develop, in informal groups and minor clubs and organizations, and deeply felt relations between persons develop in them. High standards of competence are set in certain areas like sports or stagecraft, or in courses dealing with deep concerns of adolescents, because the youngsters will settle for nothing less.

Perhaps the best that can be said for the school in this respect is that it is passively lavish. It provides much good equipment and efficient administrative organization; it brings all the youngsters together and provides them a social role as students that is neutral and acceptable. If they are gifted, spontaneous, emotionally responsive, and genuinely interested in their relationship to what goes on around them, the school will like them none the better. But it nevertheless gives them a great deal to work with.

Chapter IV

THE IMPACT OF THE SCHOOL:
The Establishment of Self-Esteem

Self-appraisal is not a simple task. Much as we complain of living in a world in which man treats himself as a commodity, the usual market mechanisms do not help us here. We can never settle the matter once and for all; nor can we be satisfied with an up-to-the-minute quotation. We cannot leave the matter in the hands of others; nor can we manage to ignore their judgment in making our own, even if we scorn the basis on which they judge us.

What we must decide is perhaps *how we are valuable* rather than *how valuable we are*; the question is more qualitative than quantitative. We learn as we grow older what our specific qualities and defects are; what we can expect of ourselves, what we are good for as human beings. We learn how we affect other people and what kinds of responses to expect of them. We learn fairly accurately how we look through their eyes, but if we are at all wise we learn not to see ourselves through their eyes, but rather to accept their image of us as one guide to be considered in establishing our conception of ourselves.

In order to maintain our self-esteem, we must be able to make a fairly accurate continuing self-appraisal and to find the results acceptable. The process, though it requires honest handling of data, is wholly subjective. Self-esteem does not follow any external evaluation of our worth. Though it cannot indefinitely resist externally imposed degradation, it may stand up rather well under attack. John Brown's famous statement before his execution that he guessed he was worth more for hanging than for any other purpose was not humbly meant.

Self-esteem is therefore closely related to clarification of experience; if we do not understand clearly what we have done and what has happened to us, we have no true basis for self-esteem. This understanding, largely unconscious, is never acquired under neutral

64

circumstances. Value-judgments of our conduct and of ourselves are always transmitted with it.

In adolescence, self-esteem is a crucial problem. There is as yet little experience to base it on, and that little is a thoroughly biased sample acquired in the home and the juvenile group. There is too little diversity of experience and too little experience of detachment to permit much objectivity. The adolescent building his appraisal of himself is therefore extremely vulnerable to the feelings and judgments expressed by the persons and institutions of his immediate environment. He is even more vulnerable than a child, because people mean more to him; to a child, a cruel parent is a little more like a cruel winter—a simple though destructive fact of nature.

Adolescents lack *reserves* of self-esteem to sustain them under humiliating conditions. They cannot easily assimilate an attack on their dignity or worth, for it produces not merely resentment but intense anxiety. The self is threatened while still ill-defined and in its early stages of construction, and the boy or girl feels bewildered and somewhat disintegrated, as well as ashamed. The most destructive delinquent acts are committed by youngsters in the throes of this sort of humiliation, in efforts to preserve a sense of themselves, though the processes involved are extremely complex and varied. This was rather clearly expressed in the exceptionally tragic aftermath of a recent incident in a small-town high school. On this occasion the principal publicly paddled two insubordinate older high-school boys. They had "gotten too big for their breeches," presumably; and he cut them down to size by physical humiliation. They offered him little resistance; and they accepted his decision that their self-esteem should be attacked—and defended—in physical terms. Later in the afternoon they murdered his wife.

Adolescents are dreadfully concerned about society's appraisal of them and of their worth. It is not just that they need to feel loved, or accepted, or to have a place in the school or the church, and so on. More complex social dynamics are involved.

In a school system whose historical function has been making Americans out of immigrants' children, students are likely to find that they can only win esteem by how they look and behave, not for what they are. The effect of this is a severe form of alienation; they lose faith in their right to an independent judgment of their own worth. In this respect, the school may have been getting more danger-ous even as it has become gentler. The era when a youngster would be likely to be seriously snubbed or mocked for coming to school in odd clothes, or with a lunchbox packed with queer foreign foods, is largely past; the TV has already shown him and his parents what may acceptably be worn or eaten, and the school will probably have taken a rather strong line about accepting the interesting customs of our friendly Latin or whatever neighbors. But it is more firmly convinced than ever that its job is to teach youngsters to respond to other people's expectations. While it emphasizes the expression of personality, it conveys to the student that personality should be built on certain standard plans, superficially varied according to taste, and that expression should consist of a fairly continuously emitted code signal by which other persons can recognize what they want when they see it. If they don't want it, there must be something wrong with either the personality or the signal, and it must be changed.

What is involved here is something more than marketing orien-tation or the cult of adjustment, though these are central to the process. The point is not that the student learns to sell himself or that he abandons his integrity but that he is discouraged from using his own sense of himself—from attending to his inner voice—even in appraising himself. He may not sell himself—people usually don't, after all—but he will still have no basis for valuing himself other than the going market price. He gets no help in learning to turn to himself for support in times of adversity or for inner discipline in times of seductive prosperity. The school would disparage this as egoism and oppose it with the ruthless benevolence of a social director at a Catskill resort dealing with a reclusive guest.

The effect of this policy on the clarification of experience has been noted; as an impediment to self-esteem, it is equally bad. Ado-lescents need privacy in which to sort themselves out; they don't usually get much, and it is important that they be able to use what they do get efficiently. We complain of their tendency to form gangs that devote themselves to trivial and fruitless activity when not openly aggressive or hostile. We usually regard, to the point of oversimplifica-tion, this gang activity as an effort to gain status and esteem. Yet, in our schools and social institutions we undercut any tentative approaches to real self-sufficiency among adolescents. We interpret solitude as unpopularity, intimacy as conducive to getting too involved, colorful and original personality as a sign of emotional disorder. Gang activity is the kind of activity which our society encourages in its "teen-agers"; though we would prefer that the gang sit around drinking cokes and playing popular records in brightly lighted, cheerful rooms, which gangs are likely to find pretty boring.

The self-esteem of adolescents is threatened in the school by two intricate and quite unintended social tensions. There is, first, a matter of invidious class distinctions: of teachers and a small but dominant group of youngsters of superior social status disparaging the vast majority of working-class youngsters who attend school or who find it intolerable and drop out of it. But of far greater importance are certain patterns of value, attitude, and anxiety which are frequently encountered among teachers and school officials and which seem to be linked to their experience of life at the social level from which most school personnel are recruited. These values, attitudes, and anxieties may not be directed against the lower-status adolescent, but they are insulting to the process of adolescence itself.

In terms of the kind of status system sociologists apply to American communities, most teachers come from families judged to be working-class. Most children come from families of somewhat lower status than the teachers. The economy of the United States functions so lavishly that a plurality of its families come from working class. But a large proportion of children come from families that are below working class in social status, because the number of children in each is usually much larger.

The solid core of the school, then, is usually roughly lower-middle-class. I mean by this that the attitudes, values, and folkways of lower-middle class become established in the high school as normal operating procedure, even though a fairly complete spectrum of social class origin is usually represented among the students; among the teachers it is cut off at either end. The common-man's way of life is what the school settles for. It is most comfortable for more of the staff, and it is what a plurality of the youngsters have come to expect. The small proportion of youngsters from homes of the upper-middle class or higher status get most of the good grades, honors, and offices in the school. But they acquiesce cheerfully in the common-man pattern of the school, like industrialists in a transcontinental DC-8 tactfully foregoing bar service while flying over the Bible Belt.

The youngsters from the lowest social class have quite a different, much tougher time. Between the way of life of a lower-class home and that approved by most schoolteachers there is a considerable difference. In this difference most of the highly publicized incidents of asphalt jungle life have their origin. The occasional bloody conflicts that ensue disrupt the operation of the school less than the publicity would lead one to expect, because the lower-class kids' outbreaks are quickly and thoroughly crushed. These youngsters are handy with their fists and worse; but they are helpless in the meshes of middle-class administrative procedure and are rapidly neutralized and eliminated by it. They too find the school a jungle and, like most fierce and warlike people, are accustomed to more open country. They quickly learn that the most terrifying creatures are those whose bite passes unnoticed at the time and later swells, festers, and paralyzes; they cannot defend themselves against the covert, lingering hostility of teachers and school administrators. This jungle is not for their kind of life and offers them little inducement to learn to survive in it. They get out as quickly as they can, often a good deal the worse for the experience.

The fate of the lower-status student in the school system has been studied intensively, though findings must be generalized as cautiously as with most social research. Schools are different; different kinds of youngsters receive social approval in different parts of the country and even in different schools in the same city, depending on the social groups that dominate the district. Our economy and social structure have changed radically since some of the classical research on the impact of social class on adolescence was done. Since 1949, for example, when A. B. Hollingshead's invaluable *Elmtown's Youth** was published, the whole relationship between small towns and nearby metropolises has been altered by the suburban explosion; while technological progress has sharply reduced the relative size and significance of the blue-collar working class. Anyone using *Elmtown's Youth* as a descriptively accurate guide to present conditions would have to weigh these changes very heavily.

* New York: John Wiley.

But if *Elmtown's Youth* and other earlier studies can no longer be taken literally, they can still be taken seriously; the basic issues and underlying values and social processes that they deal with remain distressingly strong. The really important generalizations drawn from them have been confirmed in principle, though modified in detail, by the work that has since been done. The high school still reflects and transmits faithfully the esteem or disparagement in which the community holds its students and their families. *All* aspects of a youngster's life in high school—not just his social life outside the classroom—are strongly influenced by his family's social status. Lower-status youngsters, in turn, come to perceive the school as exclusively concerned with socioeconomic status; unless they want to use it to get ahead, they have no interest in it and expect it to have none in them. In the United States, education, as distinct from earning a secure place for oneself, is a highly controversial matter in which the school tries not to get too involved.

Unless one regards the way of life of the American middle classes as a Given of the Natural Order, Hollingshead's findings certainly make it impossible to view the high school as the friendly home of dignity and opportunity for all. It seems reasonable that cliques and sororities or fraternities are usually made up of youngsters of similar backgrounds, because youngsters with a similar background are likely to share not only common tastes and values, but common unconscious and emphatic responses as well. They are more comfortable with one another in the absence of strangers. But students from higher-status homes consistently make better grades. They consistently get more scholarships than students with equally high grades who come from "poorer" homes. They are so much more likely to stay in school and finish it than lower-status youngsters are that sociologists commonly use "level of school achieved" as one of the sharpest single indices of adult social status.

The lower-status kids' reasons for leaving are sometimes hard to refute: Hollingshead's* sparse account of the beating given two "canal rat" boys in the gymnasium under the principal's supervision, while the high-school band played "the usual serenade" to drown out the noise, tends to stick in the mind. Only athletics tends to be an exception. Skillful boys make the team in spite of "poor" home

* *Ibid.*, p. 356.

backgrounds, for in the American *ethos* victory is not to be trifled with even for the sake of preserving the social order. For the lower-status star, athletic skill may even open the way to social mobility (though superior social status also makes it more likely that a boy's athletic skill will be recognized early enough to make him a star). The merely superior player of low social status will be used on the team, but he is unlikely to find that this leads to social acceptance in the school. When the gym has been cleared for the victory dance, he would do better to join a few of his own gang in the locker room with a bottle than to try to cut in on the Queen of the Night.

Some lower-status youngsters do see the school as a resource and turn to it for help. Whether they get it depends on the kind of help they want. Conceivably—and especially if they are bright— these youngsters might want the school to help them better understand the meaning of their own lives. But this would be highly unrealistic; and it is not, in fact, what these youngsters expect. They look to the school for aid only if they plan to seek a higher status and economic level—an acceptable enough purpose, to be sure, but neither the sole nor necessarily the most worthy function of education. Bright boys turn to the school for help in becoming bright young men, and not for other things they might want to do—such as lead wiser and more perceptive lives.

This perception of the school has been demonstrated in a brilliant, small-sample study by Joseph Kahl.* From among the many subjects participating in a large-scale examination of the processes of social mobility in a New England city, Kahl selected just a dozen pair of high-school boys for intensive study. All these boys were from the "common-man" social level; their fathers were skilled or semi-skilled laborers or minor clerical workers. All were of superior intelligence and in the upper quartile of their high-school class; all, that is, could have been reasonably certain of admission to college had they chosen to continue their education beyond high school.

All had made their decision; that was the basis for their inclusion in Kahl's study. Each boy who had decided to go to college was paired with one who had as definitely decided not to do so. Seeking

* Joseph A. Kahl, "Educational and Occupational Aspirations of 'Common-Man' Boys," *Harvard Educational Review*, Vol. XXIII, No. 3 (Summer, 1953).

to discover what had made the difference, Kahl found that the distinguishing factor, and the only one, was the student's attitude toward social mobility. Those who were headed for college were interested in a better job and a better position in society than their parents had had; those who were not headed for college expected to live at their family's present level. Some of these nonmobile boys and their families expressed vague longings or isolated feelings of dissatisfaction with their "common-man" life, but they had nevertheless firmly decided against the hazards and continued adaptations demanded by upward social mobility, though they had, on the books at least, the requisite capacity for undertaking it.

The school had played a crucial role in the decisions of several of these boys; its encouragement had often led the family to decide to make the sacrifices that would be necessary if they were to help their son get ahead. In certain of Kahl's families, the brother of a boy who had decided to go on to college had received no encouragement from the school and hence none from the family, and was settling down to his accustomed life. "I suppose they figure," one of these observed without resentment, "if ya got it, ya got it; if ya haven't, ya haven't."

But to none of these gifted boys of common-man families had the school managed or, indeed, so far as Kahl could find, even attempted to suggest any value in continued education other than economic and social advancement. "School and the possibility of college," Kahl reports, "were viewed by all the boys as steps to jobs. None was interested in learning for the subtle pleasure it can offer; none crave intellectual understanding for its own sake. . . . There were no cases in which the boy found in schoolwork sufficient intellectual satisfactions to supply its own motivation. And there were no cases where a sympathetic and understanding teacher had successfully stimulated a boy to high aspirations."

The most tragic thing that happens to lower-status youngsters in school is that they learn to accept the prevailing judgment of their worth. They accept and internalize the social verdict on themselves. If they did not, if they could inwardly state their own terms, the influence of the school would still be highly undemocratic, but it would have much less effect on self-esteem. The lower-class adolescent would be much less humiliated by discrimination against himself if he could come to school with a strong conviction that his own social class and its way of life were worthwhile. He seldom has this confidence, however, because the school is merely the latest in a series of social institutions—beginning with his home—that have been transmitting to him the same appraisal of himself. This, after all, is what social status means.

The most elegant study of the way school children introject community judgments of themselves and their families is still that which Bernice Neugarten* made, of essentially the same population of Elmtown (she called it Jonesville) youngsters that Hollingshead had used. Because she wanted to study the development of awareness of social status, and because she expected that juveniles would be less conscious of status differences than adolescents or adults, she began with elementary-school pupils and then extended her sample to include high-school students. In a form of written questionnaire, she asked her subjects to name other children in their group whom they thought of as good-looking or ugly; smart or dull; neat and clean, or dirty and unkempt; usually honest, or a cheat and a liar; and so forth. She also asked them to name their best friend—not who they wanted for a "best friend," but who their best friend actually was.

Her hypothesis was not confirmed. The juvenile subjects consistently assigned the favorable traits to their superiors in status more frequently than to their social equals; they withheld favorable mention from children inferior in status to themselves. With the pejorative traits they did the exact opposite, assigning them most frequently to their status inferiors and withholding them from those above them. Except in the lowest social class, the children named members of the social classes above them as their best friends; seldom their equals and hardly ever their inferiors. There were therefore very few mutual choices of best friend, so that best friendships cannot have been very satisfying to the respectable children of Elmtown. The juveniles of the lowest social class, aware of the barrier separating them from the respectable, did name each other as best friends more frequently than they did children from higher-status families.

* Bernice Neugarten, "The Democracy of Childhood," in W. Lloyd Warner and associates, *Democracy in Jonesville* (New York: Harper, 1949).

The frightening thing about Neugarten's data is their consistency; there are virtually no exceptional cases. Her juvenile subjects were not only aware of status, they were single-mindedly absorbed in it; they seemed to notice nothing else of a more personal kind. Even youngsters who did not care about social status themselves might have good reason to designate better-class children as better dressed or, if their frame of reference were narrow enough, better mannered. But the Elmtown juvenile fell prostrate before them, finding them also neater, cleaner, better-looking, more trustworthy—awarding them everything except, in S. J. Perelman's incomparable phrase, the *Croix de Mal de Mer* with moist palms. The youngsters from the lower-status families joined just as consistently in this act of humility before the high-class kids; they did not name them as their best friends, but saw them as models of Apollonian beauty and restraint. All the children were white and most were of northern European stock—the results could not have been due to simple social stereotypy. The poorest of the respectable children were of Norwegian Lutheran backgrounds, and to the research staff they looked handsome enough and scrubbed down like the decks of a Scandinavian ship. The lowest-class youngsters came from old Anglo-Scottish unsuccessful stock or Slavic; they were less neat but no less comely physically, even according to the most conventional North American standards. Yet in their own eyes they were grossly disfigured by lack of social status; with the assistance of their peers, they managed to feel ugly and dirty.

These were the juveniles; the adolescents in Elmtown differed in their responses in only one respect, though that was significant. They behaved in exactly the same way in naming their social superiors as their best friends, and in assigning favorable traits according to strict social precedence. But they did not assign the pejorative traits according to classes. An upper-middle-class adolescent was pretty sure to impress everybody in school as unusually mannerly, well dressed, handsome, intelligent, honest, and good; many people would regard him as their best friend even though he felt particularly close to none of them. But Elmtown adolescents tended to spread the nasty characteristics around without much relationship to social status. They attributed these to youngsters in each social class with about equal frequency.

It is hard to be sure just what is involved in this difference. It is consistent, certainly, with Sullivan's contrast between juvenile brutality and narcism and the adolescent tendency to respond more to the human reality of other persons. But, by adolescence, the youngsters with the most stereotyped low-status characteristics had already been driven out of school; they were no longer there for Neugarten's subjects to rate. And while the high-school kids did not mention low-status youngsters unfavorably with greater frequency than higher-status youngsters, they did mention lower-status youngsters less frequently altogether. Low-status youngsters got few favorable mentions, and no more than their share of unfavorable, even from themselves. The colorful, swaggering rogues had found the school too hot to hold them; the quietly unassuming youngsters from poorer homes who remained seemed to have been told by their peers to "get lost," and were rather successfully complying.

Even the colorful, swaggering rogues seldom get out in time to preserve their self-esteem; and where, indeed, would *out* be? The only way they can get a makeshift shelter from the ceaseless corrosive drizzle of social disapproval is to build it themselves; when they do they find that they must use it more often as a besieged blockhouse than as a refuge. They may then become a delinquent gang. They might as well. In our major cities merely to be young and cheaply dressed, in the company of friends like yourself and in such resorts as will let you hang around, is to invite the grim attentions of the Youth Squad. The Youth Squad knows very little about civil liberty and respect for the individual; what it does know, it doesn't like.*

Juvenile delinquency serves many purposes, including that of providing sadistic adults with fantasies suited to their special tastes. For lower-status youngsters it provides an outlet for sometimes understandable hostility and a temporary redress of grievances—and something more. A delinquent gang is a little society in itself; in it, status is allotted according to values precisely the opposite of those by which middle-class adults claim to live. Juvenile delinquency, in

---

* Thus the Thirty-eighth Annual Report of the American Civil Liberties Union (July 1, 1957, to June 30, 1958) quoted "the statements of a police captain to his men to 'get tough' with suspected juvenile delinquents. 'Bring those adolescent apes into the station house and don't treat them gently,' the captain said, adding: 'I am instructing my men to treat those punks tough.'"

fact, is often a kind of social reaction-formation. It not only wreaks vengeance on the middle-class world, but sets up a counter-world of its own where black is white—sometimes, pathetically, even in racial terms. Yet this scrupulous reversal of values demonstrates its continued and essential dependency on conventional society.*

Lower-class youngsters are continually subject to intense disparagement in a school and society that demand of them social skills they have had no opportunity to acquire and that punish them for the kind of behavior that formerly brought them prestige. Even so, most of these youngsters handle their feelings without becoming aggressively hostile; they are able to coexist with middle-class institutions and lead their own lives as what William F. Whyte† called "corner boys," avoiding conflict by a certain wariness. But enough are shamed, frightened, and angered beyond endurance, and therefore strike back, to have made juvenile delinquency a social institution.

Many aspects of juvenile delinquency seem clearly class-determined: they are acts of iconoclasm against specific middle-class idols. Juvenile gangs are wantonly destructive of property; they rarely steal it for their own use. Breaking society's rules of order becomes an end in itself to which personal advantage must be sacrificed. Gang members, when functioning in role, seem driven to lie, to break important promises, or to fail to turn up on jobs that they have struggled to get. Cohen cites statements by juvenile delinquents that

* The literature of juvenile delinquency, extensive as it is, is remarkably deficient in first-rate theoretical formulations; largely, I believe, because conventional society insists that juvenile delinquency be regarded as a "problem" —that is, as something external to itself, for which it may perhaps be blamed but which cannot, by its very nature, challenge conventional values. To construct a social theory that would account for juvenile delinquency on this premise would be like setting up a conception of gravitation while insisting that the sun does not respond to the attraction of the earth, but only the other way around. To some people this would seem reasonable: the sun *is* bigger and brighter, and many people worship it.

I especially appreciate, therefore, the analysis of one sociologist who has presented a genuine social theory under which the phenomena of delinquency in lower class youth can be ordered. Much of my presentation is based on Albert K. Cohen's original and tightly reasoned *Delinquent Boys: The Culture of the Gang* (Glencoe, Ill.: The Free Press, 1955).

† *Street Corner Society* (Chicago: University of Chicago Press, 1943). Whyte's own sample group, of course, were not adolescents, but young men unemployed during the depths of the depression.

express wanton hostility toward property and order as such, though the youngsters seldom show much insight into their resentment of these as badges of their oppressors. By contrast, the "corner boys" who lack the resentful hostility of the delinquent have no apparent tendency to drift into serious delinquency, as they would if delinquency were simply an expression of the difference between middle-class and lower-class patterns of life.

The "corner boy" can go on living his own life rather calmly under adverse social conditions because he has been able to develop, to some extent, his own sense of values and his own inner sources of self-esteem. He may dislike the way the world treats him, and be hurt by it; but the school and the cops cannot strike at his roots, which are too deep and in any case elsewhere: in the love he has received from a stable home or is receiving from his girl; in the status he gets in his gang from a capacity for informal leadership or skill at sports; in real friendships. Society does do him grave injury; it dismisses him and blocks his opportunities to develop his full powers as a human being in many areas of life, interpersonal as well as vocational. But as long as he plays it cool in his own district, it cannot cut his heart out.

The "corner boy," then, differs from the lower-class juvenile delinquent not in being better attuned to middle-class folkways but in being more detached from them; ironically, it is the delinquent boy who has more feeling for the society with which he is struggling. Delinquent boys are by no means all lower-class: a rising delinquency rate among middle-class youngsters is at least one reason for the rising concern about juvenile delinquents among middle-class people. The handwriting on the picture window warns that the boy you break may be your own. But the middle-class delinquent is likely to be a different kind of boy with different kinds of problems than the lower-class delinquent; his age and his actions are similar, but not his motives and his needs. Delinquency for both boys is frequently a response to unbearable humiliation and loss of self-esteem; but the agents of this destruction for the middle-class boy are more likely to be his immediate and sustained personal relationships to parents or peers, and the terrifying emptiness of the world he must deal with, which gives him no hint of any reason why people might be valuable. Examples of the kind of thing that makes trouble for the middle-class delinquent are familiar: the anxiously striving parents, unwilling to risk self-definition because to them it means settling for what little they are and giving up vague hopes of being more; peers who, though too young to bear their own cynicism without flinching, do indeed know the price of everything and the value of nothing. It is much too simple—perhaps glib—yet also very true, to say that where the lower-status delinquent responds to what the world is, the middle-class delinquent responds to the gap between what he needs and what it is not and can never be.

In any case, it is one world and the same; and for the adolescent, the school is where he must encounter it. Class discrimination is one of the trials he may have to face, and a severe one. But it is not the only trial, nor the most severe.

As one tries to understand the whole process of adolescent socialization in the school, it becomes increasingly clear that the *specific quality* of lower-middle-class life operating through the school and its personnel is more oppressive to adolescent self-esteem than the occurrence—widespread though it is—of class discrimination as such.

The high school is an ungracious institution.

> To explain grace requires
> a curious hand. If that which is at all were not forever,
> why would those who graced the spires
> with animals and gathered there to rest, on cold luxurious
> low stone seats—a monk and monk and monk—between the thus
> ingenious roof-supports, have slaved to confuse
> grace with a kindly manner, time in which to pay a debt,
> the cure for sins, a graceful use
> of what are yet
> approved stone mullions branching out across
> the perpendiculars? *

This is its peculiar lack and the source of its treachery to adolescents. It cannot be counted on for generosity, for imagination, or for style. Its staff has on the whole too little confidence in its own dignity or judgment, and too little respect for that of others. It seldom understands how these are derived from personal experience and expressed in individual action. It is composed chiefly of individuals who have

* Marianne Moore, "The Pangolin," *Collected Poems* (New York: Macmillan, 1952), p. 120.

achieved their own basis of security by cautious attention to external norms—and these not the most generous. It does not ask of a student whether in a particular action he is being true to himself and his own nature, but whether he is doing what the school ought to expect. If he isn't, it tries to be fair—it wants very much to be fair. But it is usually too frightened.

To this ungraciousness of the school and the shallowness of its conception of dignity, I attribute its paradoxical failure to achieve among its students the norm of personality it prizes so highly. For personality conceived as a norm cannot be developed. A school that restricts freedom, invades privacy, and limits enterprise in order to promote normality is certainly not going to promote growth. Yet the average teacher or school administrator could hardly be expected to see personality development as a process of individuation; the whole process by which he himself has been selected mitigates against it.

In American society, the role of schoolteacher is the least costly and most readily available role commonly accepted as of professional status. Every community affords a large number of schoolteaching positions—more than can now be easily filled. The educational requirements for the job are high enough to be consistent with a measure of professional status, but they are very easily fulfilled. The necessary courses are offered in every local college; should a Master's degree be sought for the sake of further advancement, it may be obtained in three summers at the state university or even in night classes by those who live and teach in a town where a college or a university offering graduate work is located. This is far less taxing than what a physician, attorney, engineer, scientist, or university professor must go through in the course of acquiring his license; each must maintain at least a year and usually much more of residence and full-time work in his specialty at a university-grade institution.

There are other careers, of course, that provide status without the expense of graduate study in residence at a university: in business, industry, or finance; as a writer or artist. But these all require capital, or connections, or the temperamental ability to take great risks over long periods, or creative ability, or all these. For a young man or woman without such backing or special abilities, a schoolteaching career provides the most status in proportion to risk; he can be ninety-nine per cent certain that nobody and nothing will really get in his way so long as he is ambulatory and not an obvious grotesque. Teaching is also the only career that is never chosen blind; any young man or woman who decides to become a teacher has had twelve years of close acquaintance with teachers and the surface conditions of their lives. He knows what his future colleagues will be like, and roughly what sort of life he will live among them.

It is not in most ways as good a life as that led by other American professionals. It is poor materially; the common belief that teachers are underpaid is quite true. It is subject to controls and intrusions; outside of the large cities and the wealthier suburbs, where life tends to be less constrained, teachers cannot count on any privacy. Their dress, their politics if any, their shopping, drinking, and sleeping habits, their recreations are all treated by their neighbors as matters of public concern. The teacher is very vulnerable to malice; tenure is not worth much if it must be defended before a school board, which is itself a part of the community power structure and subject to its pressures. Tenure, in any case, protects the teacher only from the threat of being fired, not from having his life made miserable by informal disapproval and daily harassment on the job. The community can make the life of *any* of its members intolerable, of course; the point is that, in the case of a teacher, it often feels free to.

A teaching career provides security against the kinds of economic vicissitudes to which small businessmen and clerical employees are subject. The kind of security that people who are accustomed to think of themselves as working-class derive from a strong union, teachers obtain in some measure from a licentiate and tenure regulations. Public-school teaching therefore attracts a disproportionate number of persons to whom security is more important than real freedom in the conduct of their life or their professional activity. Teachers do not usually desire to rebel against the social attitudes of their community, though they may resent or fear their application to particular events in their lives; on the whole they share these attitudes and were themselves brought up to have little respect for privacy and to expect little deference to the demands of the inner life. They are more preoccupied with acquiring and maintaining small increments of status for a small investment and without much risk than with disciplined self-expression through the medium of professional competence.

Public-school teaching in the United States is not really a profession, for the idea of a profession implies at least the theoretical possibility of setting up for oneself in private practice, with the sense of personal independence this provides. It is an indigenous petty civil service, characterized by the usual gradations of rank and bureaucratic modes of organization. A civil service has its traditions, derived from the duties for which it is responsible. They may be —in the public school they are—traditions of responsibility, benevolence, and devotion to duty, and they influence the actual conduct of the school system strongly. But the traditions of a civil service are not those of chivalry; they do not emphasize courage, feeling, imagination, breadth of vision, and independence of action. In the tradition of the school, a teacher who manifested these qualities would be thought to need help in adapting himself to functioning well in a group situation. He would get lots of it.

Experience suggests that he would in any case be a rather rare teacher, and in this matter experience is supported to at least a slight extent by empirical research. There have by no means been enough dependable investigations of the personality structure of individuals who elect a teaching career to justify anything like a popular stereotype, if, indeed, such stereotypy of a group of human beings is ever justified. Most of the studies that have been made have been so designed that they did not raise crucial questions or provide significant insights. But not all; a notable exception is that of Travers, Page, Rabinowitz, and Nemovicher.*

These authors were investigating the possibilities of the Rorschach test as a means of predicting the supervisory ratings students would receive in their practice teaching. Had the Rorschach proved an efficient predictor in this study, it might possibly have been used to screen applicants for practice teaching in succeeding years, but it could not have been applied in this way to the subjects participating in the research, to whom its confidential nature was stressed. In the opening paper, authors Page and Travers asserted of the subjects:

* Robert M. Travers, Martha H. Page, William Rabinowitz, and Elinore Nemovicher, *Exploratory Studies in Teacher Personality* (Publication 14, College of the City of New York, Division of Teacher Education, Office of Research and Evaluation, 1953).

A majority of the subjects were first or second generation Americans from the less formally educated and less prosperous segments of the population and were among the first of their families to attend college. They were socially mobile, using teaching not only as an outlet for their energies and as a means of earning a living and obtaining security, but also as a step upward in the social scale.

The research group found that "the individual Rorschach records of the education students were characterized for the most part by a great deal of restraint and lack of high-level organizational ability." They observed that "the students expressed nervousness and made many comments during the course of the test, such as, 'is this right' . . . 'are you supposed to see more than one thing,' 'do other people see this' " and that the protocols showed "much color and shading shock." The authors attribute these responses

. . . not so much [to] an indication of a basic personality disturbance as [to] a rigidity in the face of the unexpected in a situation where they felt it important not to do anything "abnormal." Their responses were increasingly vague, diffuse, and stereotypes on the critical cards but only in a few instances bizarre.

It is neither astonishing nor deplorable that in the American climate of the early nineteen-fifties students should have been anxious about the purposes to which even a bona fide research study would be put. But the way in which these students expressed their anxiety was ignoble.

We do not know how far these findings can be generalized. The sample of Page *et al.* is certainly not in any statistical sense representative of teachers in training the country over. But it is taken from students preparing to teach in one of the better and better-paid school systems of the country, in which the size of the community and entrenched legislative protection give teachers an unusual degree of protection from outside interference. These young men and women were not, of course, worried about outside interference at this point, but about the possibly adverse judgment of their own supervisors, even though it was not realistically possible for any judgment against them to be recorded.

Unless this sampling turned up exceptionally timid and constrained individuals, which I cannot really believe, the processes of anxious adaptation that they illustrate are a fundamental problem affecting adolescent growth. How would these teachers affect adolescent self-esteem over years of interaction with adolescents? Or, to phrase the same question more generally, how is the way adolescents feel about themselves influenced by the fact that their schooling is administered to them by a petty civil service?

An added importance is given to these questions by the great extension of the area of life over which the school has jurisdiction. So long as the school limits itself more or less to instruction and to regulation of gross conduct at school, the civil service approach does not much impinge on self-esteem. Schoolmasters have seldom served their students as models of the heroic virtues; as arbiters merely of the course of study and of classroom or campus behavior, they remain remote from the growing self. They have little more influence upon one's basic values than a customs inspector. But when the school begins to offer extensive guidance facilities, and to assume control of student clubs and recreation under the name of "co-curricular activities," the influence on adolescent self-esteem becomes very great and, in my judgment, almost uniformly bad.

For the sake of the great bureaucratic advantages—and to the school administration they *are* great—of systematically kept records, better control of public relations, more responsible financial administration, and more continuity of leadership, the school extends its control over previously spontaneous and informal student activities. Insofar as the students need information or administrative help, this is also an advantage to them. They can get vocational guidance based on professional testing procedures; help in keeping a balanced set of accounts; tactfully given information about how to plan a party or how to dress when and where. They then have at their disposal an admirably trained bureaucracy, which is a very valuable thing to have.

But such problems as these, important as they are practically, are not the central problems involved in adolescent self-esteem. A youngster in trouble or in deep disturbance or conflict is likely to need help with many practical problems, but most of all he needs help in understanding himself and his relation to other people and institutions; he needs help in learning what his real feelings are. He faces a crisis in the formulation of his identity; his basic need is to learn enough about what he is really like, and what he really wants and needs, to permit him to make intelligent decisions about how he wants to act with respect to the available alternatives.

Such youngsters need skilled professional services, but the service they need is that of a psychotherapist, not of a petty official. A civil service, in dealing with him, is most likely to constitute itself a Ministry of Adjustment; however sophisticated its staff may be about psychodynamics, its basic interest will be in the kind of problem the student creates for the school and for other people. This will serve as the real basis for classifying him and disposing of his case. It is almost impossible for a school guidance counselor or dean really to believe that his function in dealing with a particular student may *not* be to promote adjustment, but rather to help the youngster to find rational rather than destructive *alternatives* to adjustment, in circumstances where adjustment would cruelly violate his emerging conception of himself and the basis for his self-esteem.

This is certainly not a difficulty peculiar to the school. One of the things that make a psychoanalyst's job tough is the fact that most of his patients come to him with problems of adjustment and therefore envisage solutions of adjustment. Because of their personalities, society has been clobbering them, and they are often only too anxious to give society what it wants and get it to stop if the psychoanalyst will only show them how. The psychoanalyst must resist the patient's demand for help in working out his terms of surrender and help him instead, in T. S. Eliot's phrase, in

> finding out
> What you really are. What you really feel.
> What you really are among other people.*

That psychotherapy should be devoted to the ends of adjustment, rather than growth, is a tragedy that the indomitable Freud would have found ironical; but it is perhaps inevitable in a culture in which one must have an acceptable personality to succeed, and one must succeed to have self-esteem.

* *The Cocktail Party,* Act I (New York: Harcourt, Brace, 1950), pp. 30-31.

Adjustment is what the guidance facilities of the school usually try to assess and promote. The effect of this on the self-esteem of an adolescent who needs help badly can be disastrous. He already thinks ill of himself and is miserable about what he believes to be his deficiencies. He has reason to be; we all contribute in large measure to our own difficulties; they are the difficulties of being *us*. He gets into fist fights, say, with other boys in the corridor or while waiting for class to begin, and is sent up for punishment; some of the boys he fights are the ones he most wants as friends, and he knows it. If the guidance staff can imaginatively conceive the youngster's problem, it can help him to outgrow the defensive and neurotic dynamisms that may cause most of his trouble, and contribute to his strength in dealing with those troubles that, as a man and himself, he ought to live with. This is not only a difficult and time-consuming technical specialty; it is a course of action that only a person with a deep and trustworthy respect for the integrity of adolescents can see any reason to undertake.

Lacking this respect, the guidance staff proceeds to classify the case: the boy is emotionally immature; he has problems with sibling rivalry; he comes from a broken home. He needs sympathetic and understanding handling. Warmly, the guidance worker establishes palship; gently, he helps the lad understand why he needs to be so hostile; studiously, he ignores the boy's resentment, turning if need be his ultimate cheek; patiently, he introduces him to a peer-group in which his new personality may find acceptance. Sympathetic handling, indeed; this is too often dextrous manipulation. During the course of it the guidance worker may be sustained by a glow of helpfulness, but he is rarely illuminated by any vision of his client as a unique human being. The goals of such guidance come not from the client, but from the staff member's idea of what a nice boy should be like.

The boy is now in a dangerous position. His self-image had originally been painful and distorted; otherwise he would not have come for treatment or acted in such a way as to be referred for it. It now becomes blurred and confused as well. Driven by dependency and the promise of warmth, he abandons himself further in the process of turning himself into what the school believes he ought to be. What it believes he ought to be is determined by its own values;

it cannot transcend in action its own vision of life. It quietly links his self-esteem to the attainment of the virtues of a petty bureaucracy, helping him to think well of himself, whatever his self may be, if he becomes more responsible, a better citizen, and, especially, estimable in the eyes of others.

Well, these are virtues, but even if one accepts them as virtues, this process of imparting them is a process of alienation. It takes advantage of a disturbed youngster's confusion and feeling of inferiority, cultivates his dependency, and manipulates his immediate emotional needs—sometimes even stimulating them—to evoke behavior and attitudes which are quite inconsistent with his deeper feelings. These deeper feelings must then be further repressed. The youngster's power to build his self-esteem from self-appraisal is thus further weakened; his dependency on external success and esteem strengthened.

In the arena of "student activities," the process of alienation proceeds with even greater vigor than in the guidance office; though, to be sure, the students are often better able to combat it here, since they suffer only average emotional disability and have some residual conviction that their clubs and recreation ought to be their own business. They seldom *do* combat it, however, for few occasions for conflict arise. The students are reared in the same tradition as the staff; they have no strong sense of personal privacy or *general* sense of their own dignity. They need the school's facilities and administrative services; without them, they have no place to hold a dance, no way to organize an intramural sports tournament, no basis for recognition if they wish to participate in national organizations. They find the school helpful in nearly all their contacts with it, and they have too little experience to recognize when it is significantly exceeding its moral authority. Intrusion may be resented in specific instances, as when a school refuses to permit students to wear jeans or to allow a club to invite a controversial speaker to address it. But the proportion of students who care is small, and those who try to defend the principle they believe to be at stake tend usually to pick the wrong principle.

This, I think, is rather an important and neglected point. Such few students as stand up and fight back against particular infringements of their opportunities for self-determination almost invariably do so on the grounds that their freedom has been violated. The position is difficult to maintain, since we have no viable tradition of academic freedom for students in the United States and since the school is undoubtedly very much affected by the behavior of its students. It is idle to speak of students' rights in a school system which has developed historically for the prime purpose of assimilating a large population of relatively low-status youngsters, since no rights have been established for them by contract or by custom. It is also usually fruitless to try to reach agreement as to just how nervous a nervous administration is justified in being; it has some legitimate grounds for anxiety about the consequences of uncontrolled student behavior and a great deal more power to control than students have to resist. When students try to defend their rights, their position is very vulnerable.

One usually finds when one looks into student complaints of violation that what has been violated is not so much freedom as dignity. I do not mean simply that somebody has been unnecessarily rude—quite the opposite. Assaults on dignity are usually very friendly and well-meaning—that is part of the strategy. But the action taken has been basically contemptuous of students, negligent of their real characteristics as human beings and indifferent to their needs and feelings as individuals. In the blandest possible way, they have been pushed around. They have been pitted against one another in strategically organized committees, seduced with little awards for leadership and for contributions to school life; taught gamey old political tricks for ensuring the triumph of good government; playfully spanked for displaying undue and unreasonable ardor. If this is not enough, playfulness abruptly ceases and is replaced by pious sorrow that heedless young people are ruining their chances with their record in school. The record is being very carefully kept.

Against this sort of thing, on grounds of dignity, a stand can be taken, for in the Western tradition, individual dignity is regarded as inherent. It derives from no social contract, and the school is obligated to respect it even if it has never undertaken to support it. If the school has too little understanding of the meaning of dignity to guide itself in action, its ignorance is no defense. An understanding of its students' value as human beings is an unavoidable professional obligation.

My discussion of these issues has so far been necessarily abstract. For a more vivid illustration of what is involved, I will now draw on some observations from a high-school situation which I have personally observed.

A few years ago, the university that employed me was retained by a high school of the area to make a comprehensive survey of its services. My responsibility in the survey was to assess the adequacy of the school guidance services. The school had approached the university because of difficulties which had arisen through over-crowding; so, at least, its administration perceived the problem. In the past few years the enrollment in the school had greatly increased; the chief source of this increase was a change in the character of several villages served by the school. At the time of its construction these were small settlements; but recently an entirely new pattern of commuting had arisen in the area. Skilled and semiskilled work-men from nearby small factory cities made these villages their per-manent abode. Their families represented new ethnic groups in the community—chiefly Scandinavian and Slavic.

Among these communities there had arisen a protest against the crowding and a proposal that the district be divided and a new high school erected to serve their children. The issue was presented as a question of the need to expand inadequate though costly facilities; on these terms it was opposed by the school administration and the school board. The school board had undertaken to have a school survey made in order to determine how its existing plant might be exploited more efficiently, and whether a less drastic expansion, if carefully planned, might not cost less and serve a better educational purpose than complete duplication of facilities in a second high school.

With this amiable purpose in view our survey team drove up to the school for its first visit. We arrived at the school a little before the principal and his staff expected us, so we stopped for a second breakfast at a roadside restaurant across the street from the school —a small, pleasant, undistinguished place, which I shall call Harry's. Most of the morning was spent in an orientation meeting with the principal and faculty. Following this, the members of the team who were curriculum specialists in various disciplines went to observe classes in their respective fields; the long, staggered lunch hour had already begun. There was no formal activity taking place for me to observe. Finding a room marked *Library*, I opened the door and went in. In the course of time I have occasionally learned things in libraries. I learned a great deal in this one.

The outside wall of the library was taken up largely by windows that looked out on a courtyard playground. A group of students had interrupted their noonday recreation to peer in through these windows, for a spectacle was being presented. Along the opposite wall, in the portion of the library most fully in view of these students, was a bench on which six or eight sullen, nervous-looking, rather unkempt boys squirmed; they looked so ill at ease and miserable that it was not until I had seen them in other situations that I realized most of them were young men of sixteen or seventeen who carried themselves well and were much taller than I. There were no girls among them.

Around a table in the middle of the room sat a group of much younger students who were also much more neatly dressed; their manner was solemn, and from time to time they consulted mimeographed lists lying on the table in front of them. At a desk in one corner sat a tall, dark-haired youth, whom I saw on other occasions striding magnificently through the corridors in the faded blue jeans and open sport shirt appropriate to his status as captain of the football team and an official of the student government. On this occasion, wearing a blue academic robe and mortarboard, he looked odd. On the desk before him sat a big, black Bible.

I had stumbled quite by accident on one of the regular sessions of the student court. Its purpose, as later explained to me and my assistants by the dean of boys, was to "teach the students democracy" and to "teach them right from wrong." He was proud of it; proud of the care and detail with which it had been worked out. The traditions of American jurisprudence had been cleverly adapted to the special needs of student discipline. The jury—the solemn youngsters around the table in the middle of the room—had been deprived of its function of determining guilt or innocence, though it was invariably a Blue Ribbon Jury, composed of A and B students from the freshman and sophomore classes. The judge (the dark boy in the robe and mortarboard) decided whether a defendant was guilty, if there were any decision to be made. There seldom was; pleas of not guilty were rare. After all, only students known to be guilty were brought before the jury. If they pleaded not guilty and were subsequently convicted, they were given double punishment for perjury, since they had entered their plea on the Bible.

The punishments awarded were in themselves mild—a few hours' work-detail around the school, for example—though some were educationally destructive, like requiring from a student an extra assigned theme of a stipulated number of words. These punishments were selected by the young jurors from their mimeographed list; this was their sole contribution. But the formal punishment awarded by the court was the least important of its sanctions. The arrangement of the room exposed the defendants to maximum humiliation before their fellow students. The town adjacent to the school had no newspaper of its own and used the school paper as the local journal; appearance before the court was solemnly reported there. There were other special features. Defendants had the right to summon witnesses or cross-examine; but there was no formal counsel for prosecution or defense, and a box was maintained in the office of the dean of boys in which fellow students could drop reports of offenses without exposing themselves to embarrassing confrontation. This was the normal way a boy was brought before the court.

In the absence of a plea of not guilty, there was not much scope for either prosecution or defense; what went on was a kind of insistent, whining badgering. The defendants, after their pleas of guilty, were catechized by the judge as to why they had been so stupid, hadn't they known better, why should the court think they intended to mend their ways, hadn't they known their action was against the rules. "That was pretty stupid, wasn't it?" was a fairly common question, and the court insisted on an answer. The dean of boys, ever present, would give each offender in turn a lecture, sometimes tender-tough—"I'm sure you'll know better next time, won't you, Joe"—with first offenders; sometimes waspishly indignant and shrill, with threats of reform school to come, for recidivists. Yet the offenses required considerable inflation to make them impressive. They sounded bad, but "destroying school property" could turn out to be scarring a ground-floor window sill with a shoe while trying to scuffle through it as a short cut. There was quite a controversy in the court once, I recall, about whether a boy who had knocked a doorstop off had been culpable through carelessness or through roughness; nobody thought he had torn it off intentionally, so it appeared for a while as if the opportunity to teach him right from wrong would be lost. Another frequent offense was smoking in the boys' john; there was no place in the school where students were permitted to smoke.

But the major offense, and the one about which there was most tension between the students and the school, was going over to Harry's. Harry treated the boys who were most frequently brought before the court well; they were mostly poor, and he would feed them on credit, which the school cafeteria would not; they were comfortable there. So, at breakfast, had the survey team been; Harry's had seemed unexceptionable as well as unexceptional, and it was difficult to believe that a roadhouse that had been respectable at breakfast could take on a sinister character by lunchtime. But students were forbidden to go to Harry's at any time during the school day; some of them felt that he was being driven out of business intentionally and refused to abandon him; he had fed them when they had been broke. The school, they believed, was trying to run him out of business so that the cafeteria would have no competition; it was their business where they ate lunch. The school administration, in turn, would speak of its long-suffering patience under such abuse. It had no base economic motive in restricting the students, but Harry let no-good young toughs who had dropped out of school hang around his place; they would form gangs, pick up girls from the school—the very air became tumescent with fantasies of outrage. Meanwhile, the student court continued its work.

My first task, in assessing the school's guidance facilities, was to find out how they affected the way the students felt about themselves. The purpose of guidance, after all, is to help students to see themselves clearly and realistically and to accept what they see at least as good enough to go on from. The court seemed to me to be doing something very different; to be nagging at the youngsters and publicly humiliating them, attacking and destroying their dignity and exploiting their shame in order to control their behavior. To gather evidence of the court's effect on the students who were receiving its guidance, I recorded several of its sessions and interviewed defendants immediately after they had appeared before it. I was to some degree astonished at the depth of the boys' humiliation; they had internalized judgments about themselves that seemed to me obvious trumpery.

The judge, when I interviewed him, stated that the purpose of the trial procedure was to teach the defendants right from wrong; when I asked him the basis on which he made such moral judgments, he told me that he learned the difference from the dean of boys. It seemed to me, however, that the dean of boys became a little less certain himself as the survey progressed. Defendants, despite the risk of perjury charges, were beginning to plead not guilty and to summon witnesses. The dean of boys took pains to remind the young jurors that they need not always assess their usual penalty for a particular offense, and strongly hinted that the court might appropriately demonstrate its capacity for compassion as well as for justice. But this was too much for them; in one case, I think they increased a defendant's penalty out of sheer confusion. The court seemed to be casting around for an acquittal, but was ill-designed for producing one. It finally dismissed the case against the young vandal who had knocked off the doorstop.

Chapter V

Five Exemplary Boys

In order to compare the responses of students who had different kinds of relationships to the school, and to reduce the influence of my own presence as an observer, I needed more formal evidence as to how the school's guidance policies were affecting adolescent self-esteem. I therefore designed and administered a sentence-completion instrument* to tap what I had begun to identify as the most controversial aspects of the relationship between the school and its students. This test was given to every seventh upperclassman on an alphabetical list of all students, as well as to the students I had previously interviewed and who were therefore helpful as a check on whether the test was testing properly. This sample included girls as well as boys, of course; though as a matter of informal policy—largely due, I believe, to the determined opposition of the dean of girls—girl offenders were no longer brought before the student court.

To illustrate directly how the school can affect adolescent self-

* The sentence-completion technique is one of the oldest and most useful procedures in studying an individual's perception of himself and of his situation; it has been in general use for more than thirty years and remains one of the most flexible of research techniques. Subjects who take a sentence-completion test, as the instrument is usually, though improperly, called, fill in their own free responses to a number (usually fifty or fewer) of sentence beginnings given them. These beginnings are the same for all subjects taking a particular form of the test; they may be as little as the word "I——" or the phrase "I am——" or "My mother——." They are referred to as *stubs*.

Standardized sentence-completion instruments are available for the study of personality, but this is not the instrument's greatest strength; the Rorschach and the TAT are usually better suited to finding out what an individual is like as a person, both because they are more penetrating and because they have a richer literature to help in the interpretation of results. The great usefulness of the sentence-completion technique is its *semi*-projective character. The stubs can be written to touch .on sensitive areas in the situation under study as well as on variables of personality. The results must then be interpreted without the help of standardized norms derived from a general population, and there is some loss of penetration into the depths of personality; but I know of no procedure of comparable value for suggesting the character of an individual's involvement in the situation around him, in a form that facilitates comparison and contrast to other individuals.

esteem, I have selected five students whose relationship to the school differed very widely; each shows rather clearly a particular and significant pattern of response to the school through his sentence-completion responses, which are reproduced here (pages 95-100). For brevity I have deleted certain stubs which turned out to be nearly valueless to the instrument; otherwise these results are complete and unedited.

All five individuals are boys; the girls, sheltered as they were from the school's principal guidance activity and treated by the dean of girls with professional competence according to their individual situations, produced no sentence-completion material showing much awareness of the school as an institution. It was for them simply quite a good school, and an environment favorable to their growth. A number of their responses were of great clinical interest, but none bore on the school as a source of difficulty; for the girls it was not one.

These five boys, then, were:

Peter: Peter came to my attention through the low academic and social rating given him by the school, as did many of the most interesting boys and girls. The school kept no cumulative records, but each semester it calculated a grade-point average and what it termed a citizenship rating, which was an arithmetical average of a set of scores awarded each student for such things as neatness, responsibility, etc. The correlation between these scores for the school as a whole was about 0.8.*

Peter, whose grade average was 2.7 on a scale of 5, and whose citizenship rating was 2.9, was an extraordinary boy: a strikingly handsome and intelligent upperclassman of Scandinavian extraction who had become something of a "leader of the opposition" in school. In interview he proved to be a model of controlled intensity—wary as a tiger at first, and subsequently as precise and effective in his attack.

Kurt: I never met Kurt; he was usually truant, but had not been at the school long enough to acquire a record that would come to my attention in studying the student files. He turned up by chance

---

* This is high enough to make it very likely, though by no means certain, that any student whom the school regarded as a good citizen would also have high grades, and vice versa. No correlation coefficient can be greater than one.

in the sample invited to take the sentence-completion test. His responses speak for themselves.

Bob: I first saw Bob as a defendant before the student court. He wasn't very impressive, but he was quiet and dogged; he had his own dignity. The school records showed his IQ as 85; his grade average was 1.1, his citizenship rating 2.3. His parents were low in the working class. When I interviewed him it was hard to recognize Bob as the same person. He was an impressive figure of a boy: ruggedly built, with a calm, mobile face and nothing ill-conditioned in his manner. I should have guessed his IQ at 115; certainly no less.

Thomas: The judge of the student court session I have described. (The judiciary then included one or two other members, all from the small group of youngsters of upper-middle-class families in the high school at the time.) Thomas' father was a professional man. The boy himself was captain of the local football team. During the interview he was cooperative but uneasy, which was my fault: Thomas wanted to be friendly, but was used to a great deal of approval and wasn't getting any. He behaved very well. His grade average was only 2.9, but his citizenship rating was 3.9.

Stanley: An extraordinarily successful boy. At the time of the survey, Stanley was only a few months into his sophomore year; the dean of boys considered him the most promising of the younger students in school. His grade average was 4.8, his citizenship rating 4.5. His father was a semiskilled workman in a factory in one of the nearby industrial cities; the family, which was Polish, had just moved into the school district a year or so previously.

Stanley, who was not yet fifteen, had impressed the school and the civic leaders of the adjacent small town as a remarkably responsible, clear-headed boy of superior competence. A plan he had submitted for a teen-age recreational project had been rejected with the greatest reluctance because of lack of funds, but had earned respect for its author.

I interviewed Stanley and found that I agreed completely with the dean's appraisal. There was nothing of the sycophant or eager beaver in this cool, self-sufficient, rather homely boy with an agreeable, slightly sardonic manner. At the time, I could not understand how he did it; the sentence-completion results later gave me some understanding.

Here are the stubs, and the boys' responses:

THE SENTENCE-COMPLETION RESPONSES OF FIVE STUDENTS

ANSWERS

STUB	Peter	Kurt	Bob	Thomas	Stanley
1. When I'm 30 I expect to be:	married and successful	bum	a nice fellow	married	successful in my chosen field
2. Fellows at (school) like a girl who:	acts nice and is nice	sweet and kind	very pretty	has a good reputation	is a lot of fun
3. Girls at (school) like a boy who:	is popular and good looking and has money	have money	very handsome	has money	is a lot of fun
4. A good teacher is one who:	presents class interesting and can keep the class under control	minds his own business	is square with his students	explains things	explains things well
5. It's human nature to:	love	make love	eat	love	want to better yourself
6. My father:	is an iron-worker	is a hard worker	a good man	is my best friend	is an understanding man
7. If something is called school policy here at (school), it means:	don't do it, and it isn't good for us	something to some and nothing to others	?	that it is a tradition	whatever has been decided and enforced
8. When I need help, I can usually turn to:	Kurt	Peter	my mother	my best friend	my parents

THE SENTENCE-COMPLETION RESPONSES OF FIVE STUDENTS (CONT.)

ANSWERS

STUB	Peter	Kurt	Bob	Thomas	Stanley
9. The rules around here are really made by:	the school board	me	the principle	the students	the board
10. Kids who get out of line:	ought to be carefully instructed so as not to ruin their character	should get socked in the head	should be desalpined	should be punished	ought to be made to toe the mark
11. I guess I'm:	considered a troublemaker around here	just plain crazy	dumb	in love with sports	doing all right at (school)
12. I feel proud when:	I do good in class	I get another gril	I've done something I feel proud of	we win a game	I accomplish something worth while
13. When you get into trouble here:	you go before the jury		when I go over to "Harry's"	you are taught right from wrong	it is up to you to get yourself out
14. The nicest thing about (school) is:	the friendly association between teachers and students	the sexy grils	Mr. Wilson	the sports	the things I learn there
15. What seems to me really unfair is:	jury by students	some of the school rules	not going over to Harry's	the gossip in the teachers' room	so much homework

THE SENTENCE-COMPLETION RESPONSES OF FIVE STUDENTS (CONT.)

ANSWERS

STUB	Peter	Kurt	Bob	Thomas	Stanley
16. When I feel very happy, I:	think about various things	am usually drunk	shout	have a good time	get more generous
17. I feel very happy when:	I succeed	I am drunk	?	I am with my girl	something I want to happen does
18. At home, we:	have a lot of pleasant times	act every nice	eat-sleep-drink	are broke	often watch television
19. My mother and I:	get along swell	a great budy's	are best of friends	have good clean fun	understand each other
20. When I think what the future will probably be like:	probably a war	a soldier	I cry	I worry	I wonder if I'll like it
21. Politics:	interest me	no	?	don't bother me	bore me
22. The most embarrassing thing to me is:	to say or do something by accident which I don't mean	to get caught cheating	my girl friend	when I make a bad mistake in sports	when I know I am right and cannot prove it
23. Kids need:	guidance	a good kick in the can	activitys	guidence	understanding
24. Kids should:	be taught better about sex act	keep quite	be friends	use common sense	be more considerate

THE SENTENCE-COMPLETION RESPONSES OF FIVE STUDENTS (CONT.)

ANSWERS

STUB	Peter	Kurt	Bob	Thomas	Stanley
25. When people criticize me, I:	grin and bear it	sock 'em	hit them	feel bad	do not like it
26. It's no use to:	argue without basis or sound argument	try to stay out of trouble	fight	cry	wish for something you cannot have
27. Most people think of me as:	a troublemaker around school	big dope	average guy	a sports lover	a good student
28. I'm usually punished:	justly	by the whip	not having the car	when I do something wrong	when I do something wrong
29. Love is:	the only thing that can exist anywhere	mating	for the best of people	for me	something you feel
30. When something gets me real mad, I:	usually think it out	hit it good and hard	hit them	feel bad	think of ways to solve whatever that something is
31. My best friend:	is understanding and loyal, but he does not exist	my dog	Bill T.	is my love life	is a boy
32. Nobody but a fool would:	oppose the school policy alone	spend money on Peter	shoot himself	quit school	insult teachers

THE SENTENCE-COMPLETION RESPONSES OF FIVE STUDENTS (CONT.)

ANSWERS

STUB	Peter	Kurt	Bob	Thomas	Stanley
33. The people who love me don't:	exist outside of my family	care	?	talk behind my back	there were more things to do
34. The kids here would hang together if:	we had a common goal	they ever got caught stealing cars	trouble comes	we have more social hours	there were more things to do
35. Brothers and sisters:	I have an older brother who doesn't bother with me	yes	are in the same family	should love and help each other	should get along harmoniously
36. In picking my life work, the most important thing is:	liking to do it	the amry	if you like it	money	that I like doing it
37. Our student government:	is controlled by the same group for four years	STINKS	no good	is a good thing	is a good organization
38. I'm not really very much like:	what the faculty thinks I am	what I am saying	by the teachers	some hoodalums	the average student at (school)
39. The worst thing that could happen to me is:	to be kicked out of school	fall in love again	I would Die	a broken arm	to lose my home
40. The worst thing about me is:	my lack of interest in some classes and this leads me into trouble	my line of bull	my temper	my love for myself	my temper

The Vanishing Adolescent

THE SENTENCE-COMPLETION RESPONSES OF FIVE STUDENTS (CONT.)

ANSWERS

STUB	Peter	Kurt	Bob	Thomas	Stanley
41. People are wrong if:	consider me a no-good trouble maker	I say so	?	they go against rules	they think high school kids are all fools
42. What I hate most around here:	teachers that don't know as much as the students and are afraid to admit it	these tests	the rule not going over to Harry's	homework	wasting time in classes when homework could be done then
43. Working-class people are:	the mainstay of the American government	FINE	?	good for society	the average class of people

What do these sentence-completion responses tell us? Using the evidence they provide, one could draw a brief portrait summary of each of the boys:

Peter: A fiery, intense boy; passionate and highly controlled. He does not suffer a foolish environment gladly, but he is surviving it and growing. His self is intact, but he is being forced to think less highly of himself and to reduce his claims on reality. He is shrinking a little; he has already a little less pride and love to give to the world than he once had. The world, presumably, has reason to feel that these resources are available in overabundance.

Kurt: Makes a big noise; he makes a noise like a broken boy. There are more pleasant sounds, to most ears. It might be possible to repair Kurt, if Kurt were an object. Since he is not an object, but a strong young creature in pain, this is much more difficult. Kurt will fight anybody who comes close enough to his trap hoping to get him out and clean him up a little. In any case, most of the people he knows think he ought to be there; and even if they don't, they don't know how to get him out without hurting him worse, and they don't want to risk tangling with him. Kurt agrees: why should they?

Bob: Bob is quiet, gentle, and humorous. In his own way, he is impulsive and highly emotional; with a better command of language, he might be astonished—even horrified—to discover that he had the makings of a poet. Bob's world, however, does not accept poetry from inarticulate, rugged-looking working-class boys who make low scores on intelligence tests. Bob is beginning to wonder what it *will* accept—and if he has it. Basically, this is a pretty solid boy: he is not going to pieces under anybody's blows. But he cannot keep coming back for more.

Thomas: A flourishing enterprise. His assets include a fine and handsome body, skill in sports, good manners learned in a good home, and the habit of trusting his superiors as much as he trusts anyone. The shareholders are delighted. The management, it is true, has to be left to a very young man—a boy, really—who is good at it but who sometimes doubts whether he, personally, simply as a boy, is getting much out of it for himself. There are other boys—some of them *bad* boys—who seem to get more. But as Thomas grows older, he will pay very little attention to this disconsolate doubt—for which, finally, he may have to pay a great deal.

Stanley: Stanley is not really supposed to be possible. The modern world is too harsh; there is too much confusion and too little love. Young people today cannot be expected to survive it with a healthy and realistic sense of their own worth and of the realities they must deal with. A boy as intelligent as Stanley must know this, but he *is* anyway. Of all possible emotional states, this kind of health —this steeliness of nerve and vision, combined with sensitivity and warmth—is surely the rarest. There Stanley sits, in his own habitat and his own skin, at ease in his environment and completely aware of where it leaves off and he begins.

Each of these boys has been influenced by the school in quite a different way. The self-esteem of four of the five has been seriously impaired by experiences sustained at school and elsewhere; and three of these four have handled their feelings about themselves in such a way as to confuse their sense of their own identity as well, which makes the outlook for their future growth rather poor. This does not, of course, imply that four out of five boys in this school usually suffer such injuries. Peter, Kurt, Bob, Thomas, and Stanley are presented here not as a representative sample, but as individuals who represent five distinctive and important relationships which develop rather frequently between American adolescents and their school.

Of these five relationships I find that between Peter and the school most moving; for Peter, despite keenly felt humiliation and the considerable self-doubt and anxiety resulting from it, has so far preserved himself intact as a human being. The school has lacerated his self-esteem but has not, so far, obscured his sense of himself as a person. Despite his perseverant concern at being branded "a no-good troublemaker" (stubs 11, 27, 38, 41), he has not accepted this evaluation of himself (38, 41), though his resistance to it has become desperate in quality. His attitude toward the school is mature, slightly ironic, and on the whole astonishingly positive (7, 9, 14, 32, 40, 42). He accepts a need for discipline and views the school's procedures for meting it out with detachment (4, 9, 10, 13, 28, 30) as well as skepticism (15, 37).

When we look more closely at Peter's emotional functioning, however, we begin to understand how much his maturity and self-preservation cost him. This boy is passionate and whole, with a need to give love as well as receive it; it is important to him that he be thought a valuable *source* of love as well as worth loving. Here he is in trouble; his self-esteem is being coldly stripped away. His sturdy personality continues to assert the primacy of love in human affairs —again, almost desperately (5, 29)—but he now has serious doubts about getting or giving any for himself (31, 33).

Peter's ego-strength is impressive, and it looks like the real thing: conscious control under trying circumstances that are fully recognized (10, 16, 22, 24, 25, 26, 30, 34). But it is a great pity that this intense boy should feel the need of so much control. Why are his working-class identifications (6, 43) and happy home (18, 19, 33) not letting him enjoy his good, strong feelings more by expressing them freely? Who taught Peter to "grin and bear it" when he is criticized, and to be embarrassed if he should "say or do something by accident that I don't mean," and that "Kids who get out of line *ought to be carefully instructed so as not to ruin their character*"? Why does he respond to the very general stub "Kids should," which usually elicits some kind of moralistic maxim, with "be taught better about sex act"? The defensiveness displayed here is conscious and, as such, healthy; Peter meets the hostile elements in his world with his eyes open, his mind clear, and a valid picture of himself to guide him. But he cannot quite meet his world largely and warmly, fighting and loving what there is to fight and love with all the confidence his mind, heart, and body justify. He is growing cooler and cagier.

That he knows what he is losing and misses it is implied, I would infer, by his response to Kurt. Kurt and Peter rely on each other as comrades (8); Kurt, who is not openly sentimental, gives Peter an affectionate verbal swat by his completion of "Nobody but a fool would" with "spend money on Peter" (32). Since Kurt turned up in the survey too late to be interviewed, I have no knowledge of him or of his relationship to Peter beyond what the stub responses reveal. But they reveal enough to raise a question about what possible use Peter has for Kurt, and enough to suggest the answer.

Why does Peter put up with Kurt at all? As American boys are judged, Kurt is good for nothing. He either really is a juvenile delinquent or enjoys pretending to be (7, 16, 17, 34, 38). Moreover, he accepts the valuation put on him by the school and the home; Kurt concurs in society's judgment of him and makes no appeal from it (1, 11, 26, 27). He takes lickings at home and accepts physical violence as the right way for the young to be controlled (28, 10, 23, 24), but he hits back if he can or has fantasies of doing so (25, 30). There is no confusion in Kurt's mind between sex and tenderness (3, 5, 12, 14, 29, 39); if there is a vestigial longing for tenderness (2), Kurt seems no longer to believe that he, personally, is going to get any (31, 33).

Kurt's self-esteem is shattered, and—this is more serious—the ego-structure beneath is shattered also. Allowing for adolescent bravado and hostility toward adults and the instrument itself (42); allowing for the risks involved in trying to draw such complex inferences from a single instrument without supporting data; allowing for the passage of several years between the administration of this instrument and this re-examination of it—allowing for all these, I still cannot read Kurt's responses without shuddering. They are so full of little evil signs. Kurt's attitude toward the world—in which he must, after all, function if he is to function at all—has passed beyond cynicism into nihilism (4, 7, 9). He nowhere expresses any coherent inner structure of his own; his responses seem like naked yelps and moans of anger and despair. He gives nothing, he takes nothing, he expects nothing, and he is usually punished "by the whip." We seem to have spent the past two thousand years to very little purpose.

I do not know whether Kurt's response to 38, "I'm not really very much like *what I am saying*," should be regarded as an agonized cry breaking through or a simple statement that he took the test with tongue in cheek. If he did, it matters less than he thought; the picture he drew is still his own. I am also rather concerned about the curious reversals of spelling Kurt made in 12, 14, 18, and 36. It is one of the basic axioms of projective testing that one does not pick details out to worry about just because they seem odd or grotesque. But these look like true parapraxes rather than carelessness or spelling errors. They are all alike in that pairs of letters are reversed: "amry" for "army," "gril" for "girl"—this occurs twice—and "every" for "very." They are simple, familiar words.

My hunch is that when Kurt tries to complete a stub that arouses feelings of fear or shame in him, his doubtless pretty superficial skill at spelling falters for a moment. The army and sexy girls are traditionally among the most fearful threats adolescent boys encounter, so these slips tell us nothing important. But 18 is somewhat more disturbing. "At home we *act every nice.*" Take this in conjunction with the huge capitals in Kurt's completion of 43, and it begins to look as if his family's low social status were one of the causes of Kurt's shattered self-esteem.

The contrast between Peter and Kurt is thus exceedingly great. True, both are working-class boys who are regarded as troublemakers at school; both show signs of having suffered pain and humiliation in their relationships with society (of which, for them, the school is the chief instrument); both were smarting from the school's handling of them at the time my data were gathered. But their reactions were completely different. Peter I should judge to have kept his integrity. It cost him a great deal to do so. He was obliged to examine his real position in the world and take note of other people's hostility toward him without panicking. He was obliged to live more cautiously, to diminish the claims he might have made on the basis of strength and love, to embrace no more than he could defend. He diminished them too much, and this is a wasteful mistake to make. Like many people when they are being realistic, Peter was more impressed by the disagreeable aspects of reality; he found it hard to believe that the agreeable aspects were just as real and that he himself was among them.

At the time I met him, then, Peter was already perhaps not quite the boy he might have been. But which of us, at his age, ever was; one cannot expect miracles even of self-preservation. He was a complete human being, already living his own life among other people responsibly and with an acute awareness of himself and of his relationship to them.

This cannot be said of Kurt. Kurt evidently had suffered severe internal injury to his emotional structure; he was broken. His feelings seemed to be both elemental and chaotic, and to have been torn loose within him from the structure they should have derived from an integrated personality. Yet, for this very reason they were more apparent, and apparently more freely expressed; they trailed behind him, getting him entangled in the social structure, hurting him worse and leading him to express them more violently.

This seems to be what endeared him to Peter. I do not at all imply that Peter took any sadistic satisfaction in Kurt's plight. He could hardly, at his age, have perceived it as a plight; I think he must have taken it for freedom. Kurt *was* free of the constraints Peter had imposed on himself in the interests of his own growth—free to feel lust without tenderness; free to fight back when people attacked him; free to say that a good teacher is one who "minds his own business" rather than ". . . can keep class under control" (4); free to say that "Kids need" not "guidance," as Peter did, but "A good kick in the can" (23). Peter, struggling to constrain his spontaneous feeling within socially acceptable limits, must have found joy and release in Kurt's very presence.

Yet, at some level, Peter must also have been aware of what Kurt's freedom had cost him in self-definition and self-esteem. It comes out, certainly, with a meaning beyond what Peter intended, yet one could hardly put it more succinctly.

"My best friend" (31) Peter completes: *"is understanding and loyal, but he does not exist."*

Bob is a different story altogether, though not necessarily a happier one. He is better organized than Kurt, though not as well organized as Peter. Bob is harmless and unaggressive, though by no means insensitive or lacking in warmth. Warmth and sensitivity are, in fact, conspicuous in this boy; his response to 29—"Love is *for the best of people"*—is poetry. He mentions individuals by name as people he likes (14, 31)—and this was very rare in the total sample. He expresses a certain shy self-satisfaction, undisturbed by ambition, and a lot of affection for his family (1, 6, 8, 19, 27). His attitude toward his peers is friendly and humorous (22, 24, 34). He is loyal to Harry, and was among the group of defendants I saw prosecuted before the student court for continuing to go there; this has left its mark, but Bob has taken his stand on the matter (13, 15, 37, 42). Nevertheless, like Peter and unlike Kurt, he still accepts discipline and has a certain amount of respect left for authority in principle (4, 10). He is quite spontaneous (16, 20, 25, 30), though he expresses some guilt about it (40).

Bob has, therefore, a pretty solid basis in personality; he *is* a nice fellow and doubtless still will be when he is thirty, as he expects (1). Yet the impression I have of him is of an underlying and quite fundamental sadness and a blue outlook on life. Bob strikes one as serious rather than depressed. The emotional potential of an affectionate and lovable human being is evident in him; and he is bright—no matter what the IQ test says. But the basic self-esteem just isn't there. There isn't even any manifest conflict about it; Bob acknowledges defeat (11, 20, 26). Several of his responses are very brooding and morbid (32, 34, 39); he simply rejects several opportunities to feel good about himself or his role in life (12, 17, 18, 33, 43). Most sad of all is Bob's completion of 38: "I'm not very much like *by the teachers*"; here his intense awareness of rejection has led him to misinterpret the stub completely—an error unique among the fifty-five boys and girls who took the test.

All three of these boys, then, at the time the data were gathered, had acquiesced in definitions of themselves that sold short their actual capacities for thought and feeling and threatened their future growth and development. In each case the school was implicated in their underestimation, though it is never, of course, solely responsible; the home, the community, and the boy himself in his response to injurious treatment all contributed to this misfortune. I am inclined to blame the school more than other contributors, not because I believe it was the most damaging influence these boys encountered— I doubt that it was—but because I hold it *professionally* responsible for the development of its students. Poisoning is in any event an unpleasant act; but it is a crime particularly unsuited to physicians and cooks, in whom it quite justifiably undermines public confidence.

It is with some anticipation of relief, perhaps, that we turn to the consideration of a boy who had enjoyed nearly every official expression of approval of which the school was capable; judge of the student court, captain of the football team, a citizenship average of 3.9 on the five-point scale—which was rather high as these were distributed, though not as high as Thomas' position led me to expect. The fact that this was no higher than it was, yet much higher than Thomas' grade-point average of only 2.9—an unusual discrepancy— suggests that Thomas had some of the qualities of an authentic folk hero. He could not have been pushed into leadership by the school authorities, but must have had a large measure of popular support from his fellow students. Certainly, he closely approximated the ideal type-construct of an American "teen-age boy" sketched by Erik Erikson in *Childhood and Society:**

* New York: Norton, 1950, p. 267.

The family is Anglo-Saxon, mildly Protestant, of the white-collar class. This type of boy is tall, thin, muscular in his body build. . . . His goals are vaguely defined. They have something to do with action and motion. His ideal prototypes in the world of sports seem to fill such needs as disciplined locomotion; fairness in aggression; calm exhibitionism; and dormant masculine sexuality. Neurotic anxiety is avoided by concentration on limited goals with circumscribed laws. Psychoanalytically speaking, the dominant defense mechanism is ego restriction.

What sort of boy would have been able to win this much status in this school? And how would he respond to the fact of having status? Thomas surely does not bite the hands that stroke and feed him. He is completely uncritical of the school's way of life and view of life. He identifies with it, and ascribes—and with some reason— its sanctions to his peers rather than to the school authorities; he accepts the school's view of morality as his own (7, 9, 13, 28, 32, 37, 41). He does not identify at all with the miscreant youths it is his function to punish (10, 24, 38, 41); in this his attitude is identical with that of Elmtown's upper-status students. His completion of 43— "Working-class people are *good for society*"—seems, in the context, smug.

If Thomas were conceited and self-satisfied, he could hardly be blamed for believing the nice things about himself that nearly everybody tells him. But he doesn't. He seems rather to feel himself under attack, and to feel absolutely helpless to do anything about it except "feel bad" (15, 25, 26, 30). His response to 40—"The worst thing about me is *my love for myself*"—is pathetic and troubling, even to people who have not read Erich Fromm, and in a measure ironic. For Thomas has very little love for himself—far less than the school has for him.

Thomas has no clear conception of what kind of a person he is; he has not defined himself in subjective terms. This boy is no egoist; he has one of the weakest egos in the sample. It is tragically ironical that Thomas—who self-righteously completes 38, "I'm not very much like *some hoodalums*"—should turn out to be very much like Kurt in those of his responses that indicate a high degree of alienation. Notice their responses to 16, 22, 29, and 36, in contrast to those of the other three boys. Only Kurt and Thomas respond to ideas of happiness, shame, love, or important career satisfactions entirely in terms of externals; the other three boys respond in terms of their feelings, though Bob's vocabulary does not let him get complicated about it.

Most curious of all is Thomas' response to his success in sports. This does provide him, as Erikson's model suggests, with an ideal prototype on which to model himself. It is the total manifest content of his conception of himself. About all Thomas knows about Thomas is that he is good at sports, loves sports, and depends on success in sports for his self-esteem (11, 12, 14, 22, 27, 39). Now, sporting competence is one of the most useful and effective forms of adolescent competence in the crucial adolescent task of self-definition; I have already used basketball as an example of the kind of experience through which boys sometimes achieve an almost mystically intense sense of being. This is just what Thomas needs in order to grow into a first-rate human; even if he became as cruelly arrogant as a young Asiatic prince in the process, it would be a beginning. He could straighten out later, after he had fully realized that the person who was so good at sports was himself, but not the whole of himself.

This is just what is absent. Thomas apparently regards his body as capital goods that had somehow come under his control. As a physical operation he is superb and knows it. His body earns him all the satisfactions he gets: status, victory, recognition, what he calls love (29, 31), though this seems very different from what Peter and Bob call love. The worst thing he can imagine happening to him is that a relatively minor and reparable part of his body might get broken (39). It seems to be nearly all he possesses. He exploits it, he takes good care of it, but it does not seem to have occurred to him that he could live in it himself.

It is a commonplace that success does not necessarily bring happiness nor status security; that the oppressor enjoys no more freedom than the oppressed, and is lucky if he can enjoy anything at all. Yet it is chilling to find that this holds true precisely and rigorously even in the affairs of the very young. Adolescents need self-esteem whether they have been nice boys or not. Peter and Bob had solid selves, but too little esteem with which to fulfill themselves; Thomas had plenty of sources of esteem but no self to put it in that would hold it; Kurt had nothing. Does this exhaust the possibilities?

No, it does not, though it narrows them considerably. Among the fifty-five students in the sample who took the sentence-completion test, there was one—Stanley—whose success, even as a high-school sophomore, seems rooted with complete firmness in authentic personal character. One in fifty-five, as things go today, seems a pretty high proportion; but Stanley was not chosen at random; he was among the boys interviewed at the suggestion of the dean of boys, who was justifiably proud of him.

Stanley is indeed a remarkable individual, the purest example of conscious self-direction I have encountered in twenty years of teaching and research. He shows in his responses the kind of mental structure people spend five years and fifteen thousand dollars trying to achieve through psychoanalysis, and he shows it better. His mind is clear and perceptive; he knows exactly who he is and how he is doing. That he is satisfied with himself (1, 11, 27, 41) is the furthest thing possible from blind conceit; it is an aspect of Stanley's acute perception of reality; it is warranted by the facts.

This boy shows some depth of feeling, though not Peter's passionate intensity or Bob's brooding intensity. It is difficult, however, to point it out in particular responses because it seems to be there throughout and to be subject throughout to effortless cerebral control. Freud stated as the purpose of psychoanalytic therapy that "where *id* was, there shall *ego* be"—but how often have you ever seen it there? Well, there it is; take a look at 4, 6, 20, 22, 23, 25, and 30. Stanley reflects; he simply assumes that the function of the mind is understanding, and that the function of understanding is to *guide* feeling—not to supplant it.

There is insight here, and detachment. Stanley's responses to 16, "When I feel very happy *I get more generous*," and 17, "I feel very happy when *something I want to happen does*," taken together, seem to me almost incredible in a fourteen-year-old boy. His cool discrimination between situations worthy of emotional investment, like his home (6, 8, 19, 39)—though he deals with that coolly enough in 18—and the school is equally remarkable. The school is an instrument he is using for his own purposes. He is ambitious, and aware that he is (1, 5, 12, 42, 43); he knows where he is going (36), and he is using the school to get there. He could not possibly rebel against it because he does not attribute to it any authority over him as a person. It is a situation that he adapts to his own use. In order to do this, he must see it clearly and without sentimentality (7, 9, 26), but he need not identify with it at all. If any conflict should arise, it will not be of Stanley's seeking (10, 32); but he expects that he would be able to handle himself in the situation (13, 30, 41).

Paradoxically, Stanley, the youngest, smallest, least colorful, and least obtrusive of these five boys, is psychodynamically the most active—or anyway, the least passive. Only Stanley, when he thinks what the future will probably be like (20), wonders if he will like it. The others cry, or worry, or frighten themselves with military fantasies. Stanley probably will not like it; if he doesn't, he will try to change it. He may succeed.

But Stanley *can* be active. He is literally self-confident—that is, he has a self that he understands and in which he is confident. He is literally, and in the same sense, self-reliant. He is comfortable with himself, he has a self that he can work with.

The school, however, has encouraged Stanley's self-development and granted him its highest ratings for citizenship and its highest grades—much higher even than Thomas, the star athlete and Big Man on Campus. It has treated Kurt and Bob with calculated hostility and enjoyed watching them squirm. All these boys were of similarly low social status. Why did Peter, Kurt, and Bob arouse such intense antagonism, while Stanley in his full integrity became a source of pride to the school?

Obviously, the efficient cause of the difference in the school's response was that Bob, Kurt, and Peter set themselves against school regulations and broke them repeatedly, while Stanley behaved himself and used his abilities in a way the school regarded as constructive.

But how far can we accept this? I am inclined to grant that Kurt, by the time of the survey, required more patience and clinical skill than a school could reasonably be expected to supply. But not Bob and Peter; a school professionally devoted to the nurture and instruction of adolescents must see integrity as more important than obedience, and must see that a youngster who is constructing a clear and dignified self-image is engaged in very constructive activity indeed. This school, instead, chose to degrade Bob, Peter, and itself in a petty struggle to maintain its authority.

That Stanley became involved in no such struggle, even though he possessed as tough a core of individuality as any boy, is the apparent result of his exceptional detachment and complete lack of sentimentality. These made it possible for him to see and accept the school for what it was, to demand nothing of it that would disturb the people who were running it, and still to use it to his own best advantage. It makes any social situation easier and more comfortable if some of the people involved in it can behave with consistent maturity and presence of mind, and it is wholly to Stanley's credit that he could do so, as well as quite a break for the school.

Yet Stanley's kind of integrity is not the only kind that is useful; and it is in a measure unfortunate that, since this pattern does lead to success and ultimately to some degree of power, it tends to be the kind one finds, if one finds any at all. I have noted, for example, a very similar pattern of relationship between successful graduate students and their university in an earlier publication:*

Perhaps the most common characteristic among our unsuccessful students is the feeling that the university is the relatively active agent in their relationship to it, and they the relatively passive beneficiary—or victim. This seems much more important even than acceptance of, or identification with, the university's official purposes. . . . By no means all the successful students agree with the university or even have much interest in its aims. But by and large . . . the successful students *do* have coherent, personal, *intellectual* purposes which they conceive as goals and actively seek. They use the university as they might the Pennsylvania Railroad as an institution which will help them get where they wish to go. . . . They do not deny, nor are they deterred by, its occasional roughness and frequently poor service. They criticize it freely. But they employ it, at their convenience, for purposes of their own which are consistent with, and related to, its function.

So they did: but the capacity to do this is more to be expected from them; their mean age was more than twice Stanley's. I feel certain that Stanley, if he goes to graduate school, will find himself as successful there as in high school, and the certainty is pleasant. So

* E. Z. Friedenberg and Julius A. Roth, *Self-Perception in the University; A Study of Successful and Unsuccessful Graduate Students*. Supplementary Educational Monographs, LXXX (Chicago: University of Chcago Press, 1954), p. 71.

might Peter and Bob, if the school had helped them learn their own value rather than disparaged them.

Instead, it wasted their time; it wasted them. Boys of Bob and Peter's social class seldom end up with a Ph.D., though quite a large proportion of Ph.D.'s were once boys of their class. But whatever their destiny, they had a right as human beings to expect assistance rather than embarrassment from the school in meeting it, in making the most of themselves. Society, equally, has a right to expect its agent to discharge its stewardship more flexibly and more perceptively, recognizing Bob and Peter at their full value and augmenting it by educating them up to it.

I do not mean to write off Kurt or Thomas. Kurt's intransigence makes it harder to do anything with him and less likely that a school will have on its staff anybody skillful enough to try, but it does not impair his basic right to respect and development as a human being. Nor does Thomas' success release the school from its obligation toward him. If anything, it increases the school's complicity; Thomas is intelligent and attractive and has real social skills, real problems, and real potentialities. The school, by using him for *its* purposes, and encouraging him to accept its approval and that of his peers as evidence that he is achieving his own purposes, is alienating him from himself. It is not doing this alone; Thomas' friends and probably his family are helping, and Thomas is willing. But it is taking part in the social process that keeps Thomas from finding himself. Kurt and Thomas are important too; if it is Bob and Peter, especially, whose memory clouds my pleasure in recalling Stanley, it is only because it would have been so easy to take the warmth and honesty of feeling they were ready to give, and we all need it so badly.

Chapter VI

The Role of the Adolescent in Adult Imagery and Feeling

The picture I have drawn in the preceding chapters is unpleasant: specific emotional processes lead to self-understanding and self-esteem among adolescents; and the school frustrates just these processes in many of the youngsters with whom it deals. In doing so, the school releases no evil genius of its own, but expresses an attitude toward adolescence that pervades our society. I should like now to examine some of the reasons why this may be so.

For this purpose, our discussion must assume a new focus. I have been concerned thus far with the adolescent's personal response to his experience in his milieu; and this remains the ultimate interest of any study of adolescence. But adolescents and adolescent groups respond as they do in very large part because of the way adults and adult social institutions respond to *them*. This is a matter that involves far more than the adolescents, and much that ought not really to concern them at all.

Young people today find themselves very often used as something between a charade and a Thematic Apperception Test. Adults read their own hopes and fears into the actions of adolescents, and project onto them their own conflicts, values, and anxieties. They take desperate measures to protect the young from imaginary menaces, which are in fact their own fantasies, and to guide them to imagined success, which is in fact surrender. The youngsters, in their turn, respond to this mistrust with even more vigor than could reasonably have been expected, living up to adult expectations with really impressive viciousness.

It is not that adult fears are groundless, or without substantial foundation. The adolescent behavior that disturbs them really occurs, and is really disturbing. However, adult response to the way adolescents act seems often to be influenced more by the adults' own unconscious needs and tensions than by what the adolescents are actually doing. The most obvious example is the popular outcry about juvenile delinquency. Juvenile delinquency is a hideous social fact and in its present form a comparatively recent one, though today's juvenile gangs have their historical precedents.* It is hardly astonishing that it should arouse concern and indignation. But the kind of concern and indignation it arouses—the vindictive cartoons and columns in the papers, the just barely sub-pornographic accounts of gang activities, and the lusciously sadistic measures sometimes proposed for dealing with the miscreants—is neurotic, particularly in a population which has for some years endured with suspicious apathy the combined threats of lung cancer, atomic fall-out, and week-end motoring.

There is obviously something in adolescence itself that both troubles and titillates many adults. The "teen-ager" seems to have replaced the Communist as the appropriate target for public controversy and foreboding, for discussions designed less to clarify what is going on than to let people vent their fearful or hostile feelings and declare themselves on the side of order and authority. As in the case of communism, there is a great deal really to be concerned about; but the quality of the concern is as distressing as the phenomena that are supposed to have aroused it.

Adolescent personality evokes in adults conflict, anxiety, and intense hostility (usually disguised as concern), colored by a whole complex of feelings, attitudes, and influential unconscious trends. These conflicts and anxieties are erotic, in the sense that they are set off in response to adolescent sexuality and maintained by the irrational vigor of the adults' libidinal energy. But they are seldom fundamentally *about* sex. What disturbs adults about adolescents is not their sexual activity as such, but the power of their sexuality to arouse in us feelings that are very threatening. Some of these feelings are sexual; the current stereotype of the "teen-ager" includes many obviously prurient features: the tight, tight jeans; the provocative

* One of the most curious of these, surely, was the "Pinking Dindies," who flourished in Dublin during the early nineteenth century, gangs of "handsome and well-made" youths, "to a man . . . skillful swordsmen," who "amused themselves by going about the place prodding at citizens with the points of swords. . . . The Dindies were too gallant to pink ladies, but the gentleman upon whose arm one walked might at any time suffer this indignity." Elizabeth Bowen, *The Shelbourne Hotel* (New York: Knopf, 1951). pp. 50-51.

gait; the conception of the basement fraternity as the scene of copulation so continuous as to defy the laws of nature. But sex, as such, is not the root of the trouble.

The most threatening feelings are certain to be deeply repressed into the unconscious; as a result, they are certain to influence action and perception with peculiar potency. But, in our culture, just what feelings are they likely to be?

First, I believe, is a fear that the adolescent will get out of the adult's control and may also throw out of control situations in which the adult is involved. This is clearly a major reason for the preoccupation of school authorities with student publications and off-campus behavior. Such fear is in part rational, because adolescent passion and skittishness do disrupt the cautiously established social arrangements of adults very seriously. The Montagues and Capulets based their social position and economic power in Verona partly upon their family feud; and they certainly were not going to yield these because two "teen-agers" had fallen in love. What is irrational is not the adult conviction that adolescents can start things that will spread into the adult world, but their panic determination to protect themselves by fencing the youngsters in rather than by sharing with them a more complete understanding of what their behavior may bring about for the adult. The adult usually cannot face up to this kind of frankness, however, both because he is ashamed and because he has often involved himself in conflicting commitments that he cannot reveal. Adolescent spontaneity frightens and enrages him.

Adolescents continually disturb the rigid sentinels of the social order. The risks they take also trouble those who love them, and parents are certainly rational enough in fearing to see a son taken in delinquency or smashed up in a "chicken-race." The quality of this concern, generated by real affection, is, however, unmistakably different from that of the many adults—be they parents, judges, teachers, or irate citizens—to whom anything unplanned or disorderly is terrible simply because it is uncontrolled.

Second, and less obvious, but equally important among American adults, is a fear of aging. European and especially Asiatic critics of our culture marvel at our addiction to youthfulness and our denial of the reality of death. Elizabeth Arden does not maintain premises actually within the precincts of Forest Lawn; but no American is prepared to attend his own funeral without the services of highly skilled cosmeticians. Part of the American dream, after all, is to live long and die young.

It is no paradox, certainly, that people who are determined to stay young should resent people who actually are young. But it is rather a pity, since this resentment is the one sure way of spoiling their own chance to retain at least some qualities of youth. Those who love the young best stay young longest; if Dorian Gray had genuinely loved and respected them, he would have had no trouble with his picture. Hung in plain view, it would have faded gradually as he did, until people began to speak of them both as remarkably well preserved. Those who do not love the young, but still try to emulate them, have quite a lot of trouble with their picture of themselves. But why do they try?

The most common reason, I believe, is that we so completely link self-esteem to success. In consequence, we must pretend to ourselves as long as we can that our future lies ahead; that we still have all the time we need and have made no irremediable errors. The difficult we do immediately; the impossible may take a little longer.

Young people, who really do have their lives ahead of them, and who have not yet begun in earnest to make the least of their opportunities, are bound to arouse mixed feelings in their elders. They arouse genuine concern; it is excruciating to watch a youngster, especially one who refuses to listen to you, making what you are quite sure are serious mistakes. But at a' deeper level, it may be even more painful when he does not make them, or when they turn out not to be mistakes; when he grasps and holds what eluded you, or what you dared not touch and have dreamed of ever since.

Simple envy can be harsh enough. It becomes immeasurably worse if it undermines self-esteem, as it must in individuals who, like many of us, have been taught in childhood that only the successful are lovable. We may hate the young, then, not only for getting what we never had, but for reminding us that since we never succeeded in getting it, we have no right to self-esteem.*

* For an interesting discussion, in psychoanalytic terms, of the dynamics of this and related processes, see Gerald H. J. Pearson, M.D., *Adolescence and the Conflict of Generations* (New York: Norton, 1958), pp. 21-22.

Fear of disorder, and loss of control; fear of aging, and envy of the life not yet squandered—these lie at the root of much adult hostility to adolescence. All these emotions, so inconsistent with our picture of ourselves as the sage and benign guardians of youth, must be kept from conscious awareness, and thereby become stronger and more dangerous. They are sufficient to account for much adult petulance and meddlesomeness: for the mother who reads her daughter's mail to protect her from teen-age perils; for the teacher who patronizingly picks out grammatical errors in a theme while ruefully praising the young author for his passion and intensity. In some societies, this kind of hostility becomes stereotyped and institutionalized. Exactly this emotional quality was shown in the British film, *The Browning Version*, which presented it as the customary response of the teacher who, beneath his gruff exterior, is really devoted to his students. His warm heart—bless it!—shows through the chinks in his armor. Such films may do a sensitive job (this one did) of showing why a particular teacher needs weapons—gruffness, sarcasm, or the cane—in order to handle himself in the classroom; but they do not go into the broader cultural question of why schoolteachers are *expected* to need weapons, rather than simply to work at ease with youngsters as the man in charge of their common task. In our culture the teacher is not expected to need them; or, rather, he is faced with the conflicting expectations that he teach democratic living, be a pal, and get tough with the young punks if they try to start anything. Such incompatible demands, imposed on adults who already have reasons for hostility or ambivalence toward the young, seem almost enough to explain the conflict of generations.

Yet this account of the response of our contemporary adult world to adolescence and adolescent behavior has omitted something terribly important—something which is, in my judgment, fundamental to any understanding of the adult male's response, not because it is more significant than the factors I have been discussing, but because it enters the relationship at a much deeper level and contributes more that is profoundly irrational and destructive.

This is the fear of homosexuality, or, rather, of certain kinds of character structure of which homosexual feelings are frequently an outward symptom. Homosexuality, of course, as Clara Thompson has pointed out,* is associated with very diverse psychic processes. Many of these are the *normal* problems of adolescent development in our culture, problems that normally reach workable solutions during adolescence:

Overt homosexuality may express fear of the opposite sex, fear of adult responsibility, a need to defy authority, or an attempt to cope with hatred of or competitive attitudes toward members of one's own sex; it may represent a flight from reality into absorption into body stimulation very similar to the auto-erotic activities of the schizophrenic, or it may be a symptom of destructiveness of oneself or others. These do not exhaust the possibilities of its meaning.

Adolescent boys, I believe, reawaken these conflicts in adults. They arouse latent homosexual feelings directly, and also indirectly, by rekindling smoldering emotional processes in which homosexuality is one—though often a comparatively unimportant—symptom.

There remains, of course, the final question of why homosexual feelings are so frightening that adolescent boys can set off a chain of terror and hostility in men. This is not true at all times or in all places. There are, to be sure, many rational reasons for regarding homosexuality as a tragic misfortune; the most important of these would be valid in any culture. The basic satisfactions in life and the stability of any society are rooted in the family; there is great variation among societies as to what constitutes a family, but no matter how it is defined, it requires a certain amount of heterosexual activity to keep it going. Homosexuality, moreover, actually is *unnatural* in something more fundamental than the legal sense. It is not simply an alternative mode of sexual response; it does not establish itself permanently as any man's sexual orientation unless the natural course of his development has been altered by seriously traumatic experiences. People bitterly resent insults to their fundamental growth processes; homosexuality is, therefore, usually accompanied by extremely intense unconscious hostility—understandable hostility, to be sure, but nevertheless potentially dangerous. Furthermore, homosexuality

* Clara Thompson, "Changing Concepts of Homosexuality in Psychoanalysis," *A Study of Interpersonal Relations,* Patrick Mullahy (ed.) (New York: Hermitage Press, 1949; Thomas Nelson & Sons, successors), p. 218.

makes almost unbearable demands on personal character. Perhaps the most painful consequence is that it involves the aging homosexual in passionate love that cannot conceivably be requited—and that could not decently be accepted if it were, since a man who genuinely loves a boy cannot encourage him in a manner of life that will bring such bitter sanctions upon him.

Very few individuals, therefore, would respond without anxiety to the awareness of homosexual impulses in themselves, even if homosexuals were treated like human beings in our society; the cruelty and economic insecurity to which they are systematically exposed adds horror to a way of life that would in any case be very difficult to face. Yet the horror seems overdone; men face worse things without panic and make something useful out of the experience.

We find a deeper clue to the terror associated with homosexual impulses by noting the class structure of the society. Broadly speaking, homosexuality is considered most abhorrent in those societies which decry social stratification; it is particularly an issue when an insurgent lower-status group is aggressively pressing claims against an older and more privileged social order. In an established social group that is *not* under serious challenge, homosexual feelings are not usually strongly decried; they are often institutionalized and even, under some circumstances, regarded as noble.

But when a previously submerged social group becomes powerful enough politically to challenge the controlling group, homosexuality is rather consistently included in its bill of indictment, and the offense is regarded with peculiar loathing. There are many examples throughout history: the challenge of the Greek aristocracy by popular leaders of the time, as symbolized in the trial of Socrates; the Christian definition of homosexuality as punishable by death or torture, emerging from the very society in which the Emperor Hadrian had freely celebrated his love and grief for Antinous; the establishment in the Prussian state, as the middle class emerged to power, of punitive attitudes which, had they developed earlier, would have threatened Frederick the Great with imprisonment; the curious blending of a campaign against homosexuality into the charges that our own State Department (under Mr. Acheson's distinguished leadership) had become a fancy-pants organization unresponsive to the righteous wrath of the people.

The reason homosexuality is especially feared in an open and competitive society is, I believe, traceable to the prevalence of a particular *kind* of homosexuality. Homosexuality frequently occurs as a symptom in a character structure that is especially troublesome to this sort of society. This is the character structure known in clinical language as subject homoeroticism.* Subject-homoerotic individuals do not occur as pure types, any more than do Don Juans or altruists, but subject homoeroticism does lead to a distinctive kind of personality when it predominates.†

Subject-homoerotic men are persons who become so anxious at the threat of heterosexual relations that they have retained the erotic attitudes of immediate pre-adolescence. They then view adolescent boys and young men who are taking this next step in emotional development as extensions of themselves, identifying with them in their growing capacity to love women and in their success with them, and often taking a particular delight in their young friends' marriages. Their feeling toward young men and boys, unless it is contaminated with a great deal of self-hatred, is usually tender and protective— often over-protective, since they are by definition over-anxious people. They are not effeminate, however, and they detest effeminacy in young men; on the contrary, they use adolescent boys in fantasy as surrogates for their own submerged masculinity. They are deeply fearful and guilty about any possibility that they may impair these young men's virility; they depend on it as a substitute for their own, which they have by no means finally renounced, though they may never be able to release it from conflict.

This structure is called *subject* homoeroticism because there is, in a sense, no true external love-object—at least initially. Such men love boys as a way of loving the boy in themselves and themselves in the boy. They need have no antipathy for women and may

* Otto Fenichel, *The Psychoanalytic Theory of Neurosis* (New York: Norton, 1945), pp. 332-37, is the standard reference, and is itself annotated to primary sources.

† It should not be necessary, but may be wise, for me to affirm at this point that neither response to the adolescent in our society, nor any other social phenomenon, can be explained completely in terms of individual psychopathology or of response to it. Neither Freud nor Archimedes could have moved the earth very far by himself. Psychoanalytic theory, however, is crucial to an understanding of the critical stages of personality development—including adolescence—and of how other people respond to such changes.

have warm friends among them, but are likely to be too self-centered to pay much attention to them. The situation may be pictured very crudely by thinking of the subject-homoerotic man as virtually encapsulated—more or less intact—within the personality of, usually, his mother. While he remains basically a man, he can sustain himself emotionally only by loving those he feels she would have loved and sharing her enjoyment of them, identifying simultaneously with her and with the young males she might have cherished.

It would not be accurate to say that he remains an adolescent all his life; it is a little more accurate to say that he behaves as if he were caught in the predicament of earliest adolescence and tries to escape from it through his love for the young men he might have become. His intense identification with them may lead to an almost uncanny empathy. Since he is older, and knows more, he can see further and take more hazards into account. But he does not need to make a special effort to be broad-minded, tolerant, or friendly in order to understand and accept the adolescent's feelings. On the contrary, the subject-homoerotic male is not only able to see things from the adolescent boy's point of view, it is the point of view that seems natural to him.

One would expect, then, that subject-homoerotic men would be especially disparaged in those cultures that also make it tough on adolescents. And this, I believe, is just what we do find. But we likewise find that hostility to both adolescents and homosexual feeling is likely to be most intense in those cultures in which the struggle to achieve or maintain status has become most intense. Where a previously accepted status system is breaking down and it is possible to become a "success"—or a failure—through the quality of one's accommodation to others, homosexuality is most dreaded.

Why should homosexual attachment be especially unsettling in a society in which groups of individuals are struggling to improve their status? What is there about the emotional bond between men and adolescent boys that seriously interferes with the processes by which people get on in the world? What is there in the process of getting on in the world that requires the aspirant to deny in insistent terror any tenderness boys may inspire in him? I am not referring to the threats to a career that result from the implication of homosexuality—that would be circular reasoning—but to a fundamental conflict between the emotional structure of subject homoeroticism and the emotional demands of contemporary, bureaucratized life.

The subject-homoerotic male does not identify easily with his superiors, and does not compete freely and easily with his peers. At the root of most homosexuality* is a real terror of adult males; the predominantly subject-homoerotic adult is likely to feel this consciously as anything from mild distrust to an almost physical aversion. His feeling for his peers is likely to be both intense and ambivalent; he may see them primarily as young men to be cherished or as middle-aged men to be avoided or attacked. If he sees them as young and vigorous, he is likely to fight ardently for them, and then to become embittered as they pass him by—less because he feels defeated than because he feels abandoned. If success comes to him, pressing him ever more closely to see himself as a middle-aged man rather than a cocky young boy, it is likely to scare him out of his wits. The only kind of success he could enjoy is the kind democratic society condemns: success derived from *ascribed* status, and interpretable therefore as a sign of quasi-feudal affection and esteem—unearned, noncompetitive, and in fantasy therefore unlikely to set other males against him, while still providing him a basis for caring for them.

The subject-homoerotic individual is actually less open than his more normal colleagues to institutional appeals and loyalties. He does not identify as readily with the team as with individual athletes, and he does not love it as much. Being elaborately self-centered, he places less value than most people on things that do not concern him personally; but, conversely, he is likely to personalize his concern for things and people that are commonly vouchsafed only formal devotion. Achilles, before the death of Patroclos, was about as uninterested in the Trojan War as a military leader could be; yet afterward he made Hector's situation a statesman's nightmare before he killed him. The general who had sulked away the campaign in self-indulgent boredom at once passed beyond the reach of reason. It was not so much that he was mad with grief as that he had literally no other interests to which the mature, conscientious, responsible Trojan leader could appeal. With Ulysses—wily, statesmanlike, and a far

* Fenichel, *op. cit.*, p. 330.

more patriotic Greek—Hector might have come to terms; but Achilles cared only for himself, and the part of himself for which he cared most had been slain.

Everything I have ever read that derived from the *Iliad* portrays Hector as clearly more admirable than Achilles; the events of the narrative compel one to accept this. But the unconscious, which is also a builder of myths, cannot be compelled against its stronger tendencies. One remembers of Achilles only that he was brave and that he was vulnerable—his mother could not prevent his being either— whereas Hector, who accepted the responsibilities of leadership and tried to put reality first, has become a symbol of badgering and nagging. We know that he would be badgering and nagging if he were alive today; but we also are pretty sure he would win.

Those who have become trapped in the adolescent predicament frighten us so horribly, I believe, because they present us with the dilemma of choosing between subjectivity and objectivity, which Achilles and Hector represent in their most acute form. An Achilles grows—if he grows at all—by passing his perception of the world through the prism of his own inner life, resolving it into the components that produce a significant pattern. He gets furthest if he is rigorously honest in his treatment of external reality and avoids sentimentality; but his task is to say what reality means to *him*.

In its mature form, this is the creative act of the artist and, indeed, of the scientist; for a scientist, to achieve greatness, must have a kind of poetic insight into the realities of the natural world, as well as the maturity to subject his insight to empirical discipline. I suspect that this strong predisposition to see experience in terms of its subjective implications is the root of the curious connection between artistic (and sometimes scientific) achievement and homosexuality. It has always been difficult to account for the fact that many of the greatest artists in history should have been homosexual, since a condition that alienates the artist from relationships central to human experience is bound to work to his disadvantage. So, no doubt, it has; if we call to mind those of the great novelists whose personalities showed marked homoeroticism—such men as Proust or Henry James—we note at once that they exclude from their work major areas of human experience. But we are also struck by the subtlety and intricacy of their understanding of that experience within the limits of their power to participate in it. Their basic subjectivity, which draws them toward homosexuality, is also the source of their power to search their experience for particular meanings of universal validity.

At an earlier level of maturity, this is precisely the source of the adolescent's power to grow, and the fundamental task of his development. The central growth process in adolescence is to define the self through the clarification of experience and to establish self-esteem. What the artist must do in creating his work is very much akin to what the adolescent must do in creating himself. Both must be as honest as possible in examining what life means to them; each must be courageous enough to satisfy himself as to that meaning before permitting himself to be moved by external influences, if integrity is to be established. Integrity is the power to use your real feelings to guide your actions in a real world that is refractory and densely populated with other persons whose goals and feelings must be recognized and respected. It operates as a delicate balance between subjectivity and objectivity, passion and self-discipline.

Subjective intensity, disciplined but not repressed, lies at the heart of integrity, of artistic creativity, and of adolescence. It seems to me, in the last analysis, that *this* is what terrifies the contemporary middle-class adult most. Any individual through whom subjective intensity may intrude upon the processes of bureaucratic equilibrium is extremely threatening to our society. The subject-homoerotic male—even if he is too sick or too passive to make any creative use of his feeling—arouses these fears of disruption. Adolescence arouses the same fears, though less intensely. The adolescent boy is therefore likely to be a double threat to the insecure adult: in his own right as a creature of some intensity and a threat to order and, simply by being young, as a stimulus to repressed homosexual feeling in adult males.

This problem is not as serious for adolescent girls. Since women, even today, are still largely excluded from serious administrative roles in our culture, and from the bureaucratic systems that support them, they are permitted to retain in adult life more subjectivity than men; and the possibility of its violent eruption is less threatening. The greater subjectivity of women has been institutionalized, patronizingly, in such clichés as "women's intuition," "a woman convinced against her will . . . ," and so forth. (It is also recognized that they are more courageous than men over the long haul, and better able to stand up for what they believe in under pressure.) These are getting to be pretty old-fashioned, and must clearly disappear as women are increasingly treated like other human beings and allowed to participate in the culture as full members. But, as of now, women retain some of the freedoms of exclusion; and society is not so frightened that they will snare it in the web of their own subjectivity. It doesn't let them get close enough.

Boys have a tougher time. Many adults seem to look on all adolescent boys as potential delinquents, and to stress sexual elements in delinquency to such an extent that almost any self-respecting gang, to earn its reputation, must be goaded into displays of masculine aggression. We define the delinquent boy in terms of what have come to be virtually secondary sexual characteristics; the black leather jacket, tight black pants, sideburns, and so forth, have somehow become in themselves symbols of evil to persons whose concern about delinquency has taken on a note of hysteria. *Life,* in its issue of September 9, 1957, replaced its traditional cover photograph with a lurid painting of "A New York Street Gang"; apparently, no actual gang that might have been photographed could satisfy its readers' apprehensions.

The process, moreover, starts a genuinely vicious circle. Adolescents in our culture are even more fearful of their own passivity and homoerotic impulses than adults; they adapt to the fears that surround them and respond with intense anxiety and pseudo-masculine brutality. This is frequently explicit; a snarling "D'you think we're a bunch of fags, or somethin'?" is quite a characteristic rejoinder to inexpertly advanced suggestions that gang members behave less destructively. They do wear gaudy, "butch" clothes and commit gaudy, "butch" outrages—partly in response to unconscious popular demand. They act out, not inexpertly, the rituals imposed by an anxious culture.

Adults, confronted by such behavior, usually call it rebellion. They see the adolescent as a petulant Sampson, beating his fists blindly against the pillars of society; and they think he ought to have his ducktail clipped again. This is, to be sure, a rather Philistine point of view. It is also a mistaken one.

Rebellion, to me, means a revolt against an authority whose legitimacy the rebel concedes, though he may object to it as unjust or arbitrary. The rebel may hope to overthrow it, or to exact concessions from it, or to be quelled by it, or to surrender to it—in any case, to quiet his conflict about it and get some peace. Convicts in prisons sometimes truly rebel; so do small boys temporarily discomfited by rage, who want to be reassured that there is somebody around to stop them before they go too far. Adolescents sometimes truly rebel, too, against restrictions that they find unjust or onerous. But this is not juvenile delinquency; this happens in the best of families—not the worst. And it is not the emotional state of the kind of adolescent who most troubles society, and whom society calls a "rebel without a cause."

This youngster is likely to be enraged and in a panic also, though he can usually learn to play it cool. But he is no rebel, because he is enraged not at the tyranny of adults but at their blandness, their weakness, their emptiness. He has no faith in the legitimacy of authority; he has never experienced any authority. He may very well have experienced brutality at the hands of people who believed that they were exercising authority; this must certainly have confirmed his suspicions that they did not know what it was. During the beating they showed no feeling; afterward, they took no responsibility. They just left you alone, with nothing to rebel for, and nothing to rebel against, except the feeling that you are nothing, too.

Rebellion would be a lot cozier than this feeling that one has been gutted, that one is trapped, because there are no possibilities in humanity itself. For our society, the real danger of this state of mind is the very opposite of rebellion. Young men in this condition are far more likely to quest in panic for authority and to make fatal errors about where to find it. Fascist youth movements at their inception—before they, too, have been bureaucratized and domesticated— are made up of boys in this frame of mind; afterward, when they have been organized and expanded to include more restrained and better disciplined types, they are worse. The SA of Hitler's early days seems to have been the former kind of organization; it yielded power, rather rapidly, to the more dispassionate SS.

Yet, serious as this condition is, it is not unfamiliar; and we do, as individuals, *know* how to treat adolescents who suffer from it.

This is the classical existential panic—the true Kierkegaardian *Angst* —and it often yields to the kind of tender-tough acceptance that can break through to youngsters. They need adults who can accept them for what they are, without for a moment forgetting how much more they might be. They need restraint. They need to be helped quietly back into touch with their own feelings; and even the strongest may need someone who can stand with him when he first lets his guard down and finds out that the feelings he feared are even more painful than he expected. A thoroughly humane and professional sociologist, attached to the staff of one of the better-run state reformatories for recidivist boys, expressed this rather clearly: the best sign that he was getting somewhere in rehabilitating a boy, he told me, was often that the boy—in every case, a tough, second-or-more offender— would burst into uncontrollable weeping during an interview. These were not tears of repentance and remorse—the man is neither a sadist nor a fool—but simply of pain; the boy was daring to feel once again, even though he was hurting.

But, of course, it is the very fact that our society does not act on its knowledge of youngsters and their needs that creates the problem in the first place. Enough adults fear and resent adolescence to insure that it will put barriers in the way of feeling rather than help to free it. We do so indiscriminately—with "normal" adolescents as well as with youngsters who have already offended society.

Consider, for example, the current controversy over "going steady." Many groups, especially those associated with the Roman Catholic Church, have opposed "going steady"; it is forbidden to students in many parochial schools. Parents in discussion groups* that have dealt with the issue express concern that "going steady" may be conducive to sexual intimacy and may dangerously narrow the possibilities from among whom a spouse may be chosen. Whether it does either of these things is certainly open to debate, and to very little else, since nobody knows and the problem is a difficult one to attack by rigorously designed research procedures. But what is

* *Life,* September 9, 1957. The two features advertised on the cover, which depicted the "New York Street Gang," are: "Beginning a major 'Life' series CRIME IN THE U.S." and "Parents and Teen-Agers Debate 'Going Steady.' "

evident is that parents or school officials who deplore "going steady" for such reasons set a low value on the contribution of deep and intimate human relationships to adolescent growth. We do have enough research from Kinsey and a host of others, as well as personal memories of high school and college, to suggest that "going steady" is not likely to add appreciably to the pressures against which technical chastity has always had to be maintained. But "going steady" does make it more likely that the relations the boy and girl establish between themselves, whether sexual or not, will have some emotional depth and uniqueness. This advantage ought to outweigh any possible risks, including the serious one that, as "going steady" becomes a fad, it too will function as a form of false personalization, and an unusually confining one. It would still be clearly preferable to the viciously competitive adolescent market, with its "rating-dating" mechanisms whose impersonal automaticity Adam Smith might well have envied.

Less important in itself, but worth considering as a further illustration, is the reaction aroused by rock and roll when it first began sweeping the country. So long as it remained a popular form of spontaneous adolescent expression, rock and roll was widely denounced. Yet rock and roll is, as the British anthropologist Geoffrey Gorer points out in a fascinating article,* "the least sexual type of social dancing which Europe [or America] has seen in the last couple of centuries; instead of a stylization of courtship, there is practically no physical contact nor opportunity for conversation; *the dance can only be performed if the pair are in good rapport before they step on to the dance floor*" (stresses mine). It became acceptable, however, as its commercial potential deprived it of spontaneity and took it out of the hands of the youngsters themselves. While rock and roll was a harmless but violent expression of adolescent feeling and physical exuberance, at times and places chosen by themselves, it was regarded as frighteningly riotous. But as it became less personal and more artificial, as Hollywood argued "Don't Knock the Rock!," as it ceased to be an outlet for adolescents' high spirits and was transformed instead into something to be sold to them, rock and roll

* Geoffrey Gorer, "Dionysus and the Welfare State," *Encounter*, IX, 3 (September, 1957).

became acceptable. Recently, one of the most fabulous of Miami Beach retreats has been advertising an "Eden Roc'n Roll Room for 'Tween Agers.'"

Ultimately, I think the large proportion of adults who dislike or distrust adolescents have feelings similar—perhaps identical—to those aroused in authoritarian personalities by discriminated social groups. Those familiar with the monumental study of *The Authoritarian Personality** will recall that the concept was first formulated in an effort to explain the dynamics of anti-Semitism and of prejudice and hostility toward other minority or subordinated groups —including women. The basic characteristics of the authoritarian personality include a high degree of generalized hostility, suspiciousness, and prurience; great constriction of spontaneous emotional expression of any kind, and its replacement with conventional sentimentality; the cloaking of a readiness to resort to violence in rationalized respectability; punitiveness justified as a defense of an orderly society; and an utter inability to empathize with weaker individuals, responding instead to their needs with fear and rage. It was found in the course of the research that individuals could be accurately classed as authoritarian to the extent that they tended to agree with a series of statements, including the following (the last quoted was scored in reverse):

"A person who has bad manners, habits, and breeding, can hardly expect to get along with decent people."

"There is hardly anything lower than a person who does not feel a great love, gratitude, and respect for his parents."

"Obedience and respect for authority are the most important virtues children should learn."

"What the youth needs most is strict discipline, rugged determination, and the will to fight for family and country."

"Homosexuals are nothing but degenerates and ought to be severely punished."

"The wild sex life of the old Greeks and Romans was tame compared to some of the goings-on in this country, even in places where people might least expect it."

"One of the main values of progressive education is that it gives the child great freedom in expressing those natural impulses and

* T. W. Adorno, *et al.* (New York: Harper, 1950).

desires so often frowned upon by conventional middle-class society." If this is correct, then "teen-agers" must be regarded as, in certain respects, another discriminated minority group. They have, to be sure, some real characteristics of their own that arouse hostility, though they do not necessarily justify it: Negroes *are* Negroes, Jews *are* Jews, and "teen-agers" *are* adolescents. Yet it is curious that common characteristics are imputed to very different groups if they fall under authoritarian censure. Here is a people that are usually carefree, exuberant, long of limb and fleet of foot. Noted for athletic and (it is whispered) sexual prowess, they are nonetheless essentially childlike, irresponsible, and given to outbursts of unrestrained violence. They are undisciplined. With the aid of jazz that they seem almost to have in their bones, they work themselves up to erotic frenzies in which they abandon themselves to utter license.

So might an embittered segregationist speak of the Negro, though he would probably be a bit more sophisticated today; this is the stereotype of thirty years ago. It would still serve without alteration as a widely acceptable description of the contemporary adolescent. But it would fit without fundamental alteration several minority groups that our culture has scorned: the fun-loving Italian, given to *vino* and *vendette*; hunky Stanley Kowalski, taking out after Blanche Dubois in the unavoidable absence of his wife. The legend recurs in our culture like a prized nightmare.

Whether these stereotypes are accurate is not the point. Let us freely grant that they refer to elements of reality; all myths do. What is a matter of concern is our need to dramatize these particular elements as a national menace, while neglecting or remaining stubbornly apathetic toward the humane and lovable features of the same persons, which often stem from the same dynamic sources. The ant, I suppose, has always hated the grasshopper, particularly if the winter is mild and the antlike virtues do not pay. But today we live in a peculiarly antlike world, less thrifty perhaps, but more cooperative. Authoritarianism is an antlike vice, characterized by pettiness and hostility, but dangerous when its protagonists are numerous.

I believe that the growth of hostility toward the adolescent is one more index of the rootlessness and barrenness of modern life; of the intense need for status in a society which provides few stable guarantees of respect on which a sense of personal worth can be based. It is quite true, of course, that, in our way of life, influence and prestige carefully accumulated in tiny increments through the years can be dissipated in a few frighteningly spontaneous gestures. And it is even truer that those of us who are most bitter are those—and they are many—who have always calculated their chances nicely and yet failed because of the very tension aroused by their aspirations.

We have today many miserable young people who sometimes behave very badly. Whether it does more good or harm to think of this as a "youth problem" or the "problem of juvenile delinquency" or whatever, I do not know. Nor do I know whether, if we persist in thinking of these young people as a problem, a solution can be found. But I do know that the only good solution must be one in which their integrity and unique characteristics can be treasured and preserved. Some must be punished, no doubt, because they are betraying their own humanity through their behavior, as well as infringing the humanity of other persons. But they must not be smoothly lured into the cooperative folkways of middle-class society, as if the world were one vast Holiday Camp, in which the most important thing was to keep those who were having a bad time from noticing it and making a fuss about it. The role of the adolescent in adult imagery and feeling is to remind us what might have been expected of adult life. If we find the recollection painful, that is our responsibility—not theirs.

Chapter VII

The Vanishing Adolescent

Many diverse elements affect the relationship of the American adolescent to other persons and to social institutions. We have examined some of these. Taken together they constitute a very complex system. Variable as these factors are, however, there is at the core of this system a single fundamental problem.

That problem is the adolescent's need to define himself under conditions which make it increasingly difficult for him to do so. The natural processes of emotional development in adolescence are regularly frustrated in our society, even in the school, which has a professional responsibility to promote healthy development. Furthermore, the adolescent may become involved in adult emotional responses that have very little to do with him as a person and that chiefly reflect the adults' inner tensions.

Throughout this analysis my position has been, on the whole, pessimistic. I have maintained that the adolescent is very frequently the victim of hostile social processes, and is himself very frequently goaded into hostile action by social processes he is hardly in a position to understand. Some youngsters suffer; but those are worse off who never form a clear conception of themselves and what they stand for. These take no stands and fight no battles; in any orchestra they play it cool. Ultimately, they fare no better; lacking purposes of their own, they are subject to discard by those who have been using them, whether these are campus politicians, leaders of delinquent gangs, or salesmen intent on developing a juvenile market.

It would be pleasant, and not unconventional, to turn in conclusion to the brighter side. Doubtless, one could be found, as the example of Stanley in Chapter V suggests. Understanding, however, is more sustaining than cheerfulness.

I believe that adolescence, as a developmental process, is becoming obsolete. The kind of personal integration which results from conflict between a growing human being and his society is no longer the mode of maturity our society cultivates. We expect—indeed, we usually demand—from adults quite a different sort of behavior than that which exemplifies a well-defined and well-established self.

This is why I said, in my first chapter, that many adolescent groups behave aristocratically in a social order hostile to aristocratic principles. This adult hostility toward adolescence frequently originates in the anxiety and resentment aroused by adolescents' capacity for intense and highly subjective experience, and for impassioned— if often inarticulate and ambivalent—personal relationships. To the adolescent, encounters with hostile and manipulative individuals and social institutions are very personal experiences that tend toward his disintegration. But to a sympathetic observer they are more than that; they are also indications of a social trend.

Homo sapiens is undergoing a fundamental model change. The Western world has been tooling up for it for some time, and it involves great alteration in the processes of personality development. A different kind of adult is being produced, representing a different conception of maturity. In order to turn him out in quantity, adolescence must become quite another sort of unit process than it was. In the school and society, the changeover is proceeding most efficiently.

The change can be described most simply as a weakening in the relationship between maturity on one hand, and stability of identity on the other. Classically, the two terms have been thought to mean almost the same thing; a grown person is, among other things, an individual who has a well-defined personality of his own and whose adaptations to his environment are conscious compromises made for his own purposes. We have not considered as mature those individuals who are driven by anxiety to accept their environment without question, making adjustment a moral value in itself. Before World War I, our schools, and the values and attitude toward life informally conveyed through popular culture, rather consistently expressed this conception of maturity and sought sometimes to coerce the adolescent into accepting it.

This conception of maturity as self-direction—and at best, as autonomy—expressed not a statistical norm, but a value-judgment in favor of the examined life of the classical tradition. Tradition, however, cannot ignore reality. As the conditions of life alter in such a way as to provide less scope for self-direction, autonomy itself either becomes suspect or must be redefined as a kind of considered acquiescence in the demands of group living. The persistence of the older ideal of maturity, then, becomes a source of conflict and *anomie,* burdening those who try to live up to it with additional self-doubt. Maturation itself, then becomes a source of anxiety from which the adult must seek refuge.

Anxiety, I suppose, is always the instrument of acculturation. Social institutions—and especially those whose purposes is to mold the character of the young—make use of it both unconsciously and deliberately to enforce the adaptations on which they depend. Still, a man is a man for all that, and it matters very much if society bars the adolescent with its moat of anxiety from just those goals of personal development that are the signal attributes of manhood. Societies have often tried to whip their young into adulthood with calculated brutality. Yet even this, intolerable as it is, probably causes less pain—and may even give rise to less brutality in the long run— than our practice of training young people to feel anxious and guilty if they allow themselves to be caught maintaining a rigid moral attitude.

The kind of consequences that disturb me are most vividly illustrated by the recent history of the United States Marine Corps. In the past few years there have been several incidents of outrageous brutality that have made international news: the drowning of recruits in the course of a punishment march and the incidents of obscene torture by Marine guards in the brig of a Naval base were the most conspicuous. Brutal physical hazing is a prized tradition of the Corps, which has tacitly encouraged it as part of its rationale of toughness. In fact, brutal physical hazing is almost ineradicable from such a program, not because it really toughens anybody up—this is doubtful—but because it discharges some of the tensions that build up when men so completely dominate boys. But what is now going on is no longer hazing, because those who inflict it seem no longer to identify themselves with the traditions of the Corps. They simply use the opportunity it provides them to act out their individual sadistic fantasies. There are therefore no limits to what they may do; the Marine Corps is at the mercy of individual psychopathology.

The decision to spend one's only life as an enlisted man in the Marines is likely, in any case, to be made preponderantly by persons of strongly sado-masochistic tendency and authoritarian character structure. But the old-line Marine sergeant was likely to have an ego as strong as his id. He knew who he was and cared who he was; he *was* the Corps. While the Corps was careful not to keep him on too short emotional rations by denying him the dirtier forms of hazing, it could count on him to maintain its integrity and respect its interests. The treatment recruits received at his hands was a genuine hazing, in the sense that those who inflicted it really did see themselves as continuing an institution to which they were wholly devoted and into which they were receiving neophytes. They enjoyed themselves in ways that the Corps would have found hard to defend publicly, but they did not enjoy themselves at the expense of the Corps and contribute to its disintegration. The recruits, similarly, could accept hazing and discipline because they knew who they were and what they wanted to be—Marines. For them, the sergeant was a model as well as a menace; perhaps to be hated, surely to be feared, almost to be loved, certainly not to be despised. When they broke discipline they were courting punishment, which has never lacked suitors. They were not scorning their role as Marine recruits.

Today, there seems to be much more cynicism, less integrity, and less depth of identification. Neither the D.I. nor the recruit has much sense of what a Marine is. The recruit is convinced that he *ought* to be able to go home to a good job and mother; the D.I. knows that no amount of hazing will shake his conviction, and that the best that can be hoped for is to make good and sure he is afraid to try it. The recruit *is* afraid; he knows what the D.I. can do to him; but he has also seen enough Marine Corps movies and TV shows to believe that the D.I. is basically phony and to suspect that the Corps is. This suggests a policy: phonies are nothing new, and not dangerous unless you spoil their show; basically, they don't want trouble either. There will be tough days ahead, but a smart boy should be able to get along, as long as he doesn't show it—and as long as he doesn't fall into the hands of a D.I. who makes atavistically the error of getting emotional, confuses everything, and ends up getting people killed.*

* *The New York Times,* in a special dispatch on the third anniversary of the Parris Island drownings, reports that the depot commander there, with-

The Marine Corps, it is said, makes a man of you, but not, apparently, the kind of man the Corps is used to. What kind does it make? We know a little more about this from the Army, which also makes men—mass-produces them—and releases more information than the Corps about the product. On October 26, 1957, *The New Yorker* published an account of "a formal study [conducted by the Defense Department] of the behavior of our Korean prisoners of war in all its aspects—medical, psychological, propagandistic, and legal. The study turned out to be a massive one—it was not completed until July 29, 1955, two years and two days after the signing of the armistice at Panmunjom.† The author of the account, Eugene Kinkead, reported that

. . . roughly one out of every three American prisoners in Korea was guilty of some sort of collaboration with the enemy, ranging from such serious offenses as writing anti-American propaganda and informing on comrades to the relatively innocuous one of broadcasting Christmas greetings home, and thereby putting the Communists in a favorable light, because such a broadcast had to include a report of good treatment at their hands. Then, when the war ended and the prisoners began to return, it became clear that some of them had behaved brutally to their fellow prisoners, and for a time the newspapers carried reports of grisly incidents in the prison camps, including the murder of Americans by other Americans. . . . Furthermore, during the entire Korean conflict not one of our men escaped from a prison camp. And, finally, to mention another calamity that might not, on the face of it, seem to point to any moral or disciplinary weakness among the prisoners, thirty-eight per cent of them—2,730 out of 7,190—died in captivity. This was a higher

out "basic changes in the Marine training philosophy," has "sternly suppressed practices 'offending against human dignity.'" He has certainly forbidden practices that were brutal and obscene. But from the *Times'* account, it appears that human dignity is not yet the characteristic motif of life on Parris Island. "Today the drill instructors, all of them sergeants, speak like psychiatrists. One hears them discuss a recruit's 'poor hostility control' and 'anti-social attitudes.' . . . A crowd of sergeants at the drill instructors school insisted they could mould recruits by 'persuasive leadership.' . . . 'It's like training a dog,' another sergeant said mildly." "Goof-offs" have been segregated in a "motivation platoon"; slow-learners in a "proficiency platoon."—— From "Marines End Brutality in Drill," by Homer Bigart, *The New York Times*, April 12, 1959; p. 1.

† Eugene Kinkead, "The Study of Something New in History," *The New Yorker*, XXXIII, No. 36, 114-69. This has recently been expanded into a highly provocative book under the title *In Every War But One* (New York: Norton, 1959). My comments are based on the original *New Yorker* article.

prisoner death rate than that in any of our previous wars, including the Revolution, in which it was estimated to have been about thirty-three per cent.

No prisoners were shot or tortured, and they received, by and large, quite adequate clothing allowances. Food, housing, and medical attention were adequate to sustain life; none of the 229 Turks who were taken prisoner died in captivity, though almost half were wounded at the time of their capture.

The difficulties lay deeper. Mr. Kinkead recounted the observations of an Army doctor, Major Clarence L. Anderson, who "was captured by the Chinese on November 3, 1950 at Unsan. After his repatriation, nearly three years later, he was awarded the Distinguished Service Cross for his heroism in rounding up the wounded there and administering first aid to them, and for his refusal to leave them when the unwounded members of his battalion pulled out in retreat. . . . During the first months of his captivity, Major Anderson was allowed by the Communists to move freely among the camp compounds and give medical attention to prisoners. Consequently, his knowledge of conditions among the prisoners was much wider than that of most captives, who knew only the men in their own squads."

"It is a sad fact, but it is a fact that the men who were captured in large groups early in the war often became unmanageable," he said. "They refused to obey orders, and they cursed and sometimes struck officers who tried to enforce orders. Naturally, the chaos was encouraged by the Communists, who told the captives immediately after they were taken that rank no longer existed among them—that they were all equal as simple prisoners of war released from capitalist bondage. At first, the badly wounded suffered most. On the marches back from the line to the temporary holding camps, casualties on litters were often callously abandoned beside the road. Able-bodied prisoners refused to carry them, even when their officers commanded them to do so. If a Communist guard ordered a litter shouldered, our men obeyed; otherwise the wounded were left to die. On the march, in the temporary camps, and in the permanent ones, the strong regularly took food from the weak. There was no discipline to prevent it. Many men were sick, and these men, instead of being helped and nursed by the others, were ignored, or worse. Dysentery was common, and it made some men too weak to walk. On winter nights, helpless men with dysentery were rolled outside the huts by their comrades and left to die in the cold."

What struck Major Anderson most forcibly was the almost universal inability of the prisoners to adjust to a primitive situation. "They lacked the old Yankee resourcefulness," he said. "This was partly—but *only* partly, I believe—the result of the psychic shock of being captured. It was also, I think, the result of some new failure in the childhood and adolescent training of our young men—a new softness." For a matter of months—until about April 1951, Anderson said—most prisoners displayed signs of shock, remaining within little shells they had created to protect them from reality. There was practically no communication among the men, and most of them withdrew into a life of inactivity. In fact, very few seemed to be interested even in providing themselves with the basic necessities of food, warmth, and shelter. The Chinese sometimes gave prisoners a chance to go up into nearby hills and bring down firewood, but the men were too lethargic to do it. The whole routine of Army life collapsed. One prisoner could not challenge another to act like a soldier, because too often the other man would say he wasn't a soldier any more. As Anderson and another doctor made their daily rounds, the one way they could even begin to arouse a sense of responsibility in the men was by urging them not to act like soldiers but like human beings—to wash once in a while, to keep their clothes and their quarters moderately clean, and to lend each other a hand sometimes. This very weak plea, Anderson said, was the only one to which there was any response at all.

This report must be interpreted with the caution customary in drawing inferences from official documents. It is based entirely on official Army sources, and seems on internal evidence to be making a propaganda point that our boys are too soft and need tougher discipline to get them into orbit. There were *no* interviews with individual ex-prisoners. But the facts on which the report is based are clear, and they do seem to bear out my belief that adolescence, as a developmental process, is becoming obsolete. The young men whose behavior in captivity so troubled Major Anderson could not have passed through a true adolescence. The picture is not wholly dark; I find it reassuring rather than saddening, for example, that the prisoners responded better to being asked to behave like human beings than like soldiers. It is more basic, after all. But there was certainly something terribly wrong with these young men: not softness, but hardness, slickness, and brittleness. I would call it ego-failure—a collapse of identity.

As Erik H. Erikson points out in *Childhood and Society,** the

* New York: Norton, 1950, p. 267.

growing American characteristically defends himself against anxiety by learning not to become too involved. Fair, decent, kindly, and humorous when not under stress, the American boy learns early that devotion can be dangerous and that feeling must be sacrificed to flexibility. "Ego-restriction," says Erikson, "saves our boy much moral wear and tear." It does not, however, save him from himself when he has only himself to go on. Kinkead cites a comment by Major Henry A. Segal, then chief of the Neuropsychiatric Consultation Service at Walter Reed Army Hospital:

"As further evidence of the success of the Communist techniques, Segal told me that most of the repatriates came home thinking of themselves not as part of a group but as isolated individuals. This emerged in their response to questions about what their service outfit had been. Where the Turks, for example, said proudly, 'Third Company, First Regiment, Turkish Volunteer Brigade,' or whatever it may have been, the Americans were likely to respond with the number of their prison camp and the company or platoon they had belonged to there."

So, ironically, rearing and social experience that stress being a good guy and getting along with the group lead to abandonment when the group is threatened or disrupted; togetherness ends in isolation. Persons like these young soldiers are often called immature —the word is applied to certain of them in the *New Yorker* account. Yet to use it is to beg the central question their conduct raises. They did not seem to be abnormal. "The Army psychiatrists had drawn certain general conclusions about the returned prisoners, Segal told me, and one was that the incidence among them of psychiatric disorders requiring hospitalization was no higher than that of the country as a whole"—this, despite their ordeal.

We may believe, and there is evidence to support our faith, that the processes of growth tend in themselves to be benign and productive, and that a man who settles for less than his full humanity is to that extent therefore immature. But the processes of growth are not the only processes that establish themselves as the human psyche develops in its culture. There are forces of alienation as well. And in a society in which they ordinarily triumph—in which what we are accustomed to call maturity becomes exceptional in itself—the word "maturity" can be a source of self-delusion.

Adolescent growth can and should lead to a completely human adulthood; defined as the development of a stable sense of self, it could lead nowhere else. I have therefore treated youngsters who do not achieve this stability as, in a sense, victims of cruelty, misfortune, or social pathology. So they are. But they are also the products of what, in our society, is normal growth; of growth, that is, consistently distorted so as to lead to the outcome society actually expects and, under ordinary circumstances, rewards.

The Korean prisoners, from this point of view, must be regarded as model Americans—a comparatively new model, though not new to America alone. We were late, indeed, getting into production; this sort of young man is a standard character in existentialist novels and post-World War II Italian films. He is Ortega's mass-man, "which sets no value on itself—good or ill—based on specific grounds, but which feels itself 'just like everybody,' and nevertheless is not concerned about it."* His face was recognizable to a conservative Spanish statesman and scholar thirty years ago.

He can never have been an adolescent, in my sense of the term. He is not likely to have had much chance to be: his society has kept those chances to a minimum, sequestering him in institutions inimical to clarity and growth, placing him in the hands of individuals themselves insufficiently characterized. Puberty occurs, to be sure, but to what sort of manhood does it lead?

We may not think much of the manhood of the recreant Korean captives. Judged by the standards we like to believe we hold, they fail. But it is we who have allowed those standards to become obsolete. In our social institutions, the kind of character structure that is actually nurtured to full development is very different from the kind we profess to esteem most highly. In the process of growing up many of our youth lose their integrity—or fail to develop it—because they actually have very little opportunity to learn that integrity is valuable, and a great deal of opportunity to learn that it is a luxury they probably cannot afford.

Can they afford it? Is it worth having in the modern world? In an extreme situation, the death rate among Korean prisoners suggests we cannot live without it. But men do not develop the qualities an

* José Ortega y Gasset, *The Revolt of the Masses* (New York: Norton, 1932), p. 15.

extreme situation demands unless those qualities are of some value in their daily lives. Human growth occurs gradually. If integrity is not encouraged from day to day, one can hardly expect men to display it in emergencies.

It must be granted that in many respects our conception of integrity is obsolete; we include in it some ways of feeling and acting that acquired their significance under social conditions that no longer exist. Individualism, which led to success in a society dominated by the economic necessities of industrialization and empire, is a poor model for the young today. Equally dysfunctional is the model of the artist or intellectual as critic and rebel. Not that criticism and rebellion have ceased to be socially useful—they are more useful than ever. But the traditional style presupposes the existence of more substantial targets than can be found in times when commitments, even to evil, are usually elusive. What does Don Quixote do when the windmills become atomic piles and go underground?

He learns to express his selfhood in different contexts and a different manner; he learns to serve honorably on committees and to perform lovingly and penetratingly the necessary acts of administration. He learns as always to respect himself and other people for their basic human qualities, but to recognize these through different clues. Even so, E. M. Forster's statement in *Two Cheers for Democracy** that

The people I respect most behave as if they were immortal and as if society was eternal. Both assumptions are false: both of them must be accepted as true if we are to go on eating and working and loving, and are to keep open a few breathing holes for the human spirit.

is still the best description of integrity I know and the best reason for thinking it indispensable.

Is there anything we can do, as a matter of policy and conscious choice, to help more people behave "as if they were immortal and as if society was eternal," instead of as the Korean prisoners behaved? This is not the kind of undertaking that succeeds easily, for integrity —or its lack—must stem from the deepest cultural roots; one is not dealing here with a problem of technique. One may fairly say, how-

* New York: Harcourt, Brace, 1951, p. 71.

ever, that whatever is done is more likely to be fruitful if its effect is to improve the conditions of adolescence than if directed toward any other stage of growth. In adolescence, the force of growth itself is most squarely on the side of integrity; it is then that development is most concerned with it.

For the school, the first step is to increase greatly the emphasis placed on competence. I mean intellectual competence, particularly, since that has been slighted by the school as well as by the rest of our culture. But the need goes deeper than that.

The significance of competence in developing a stable identity is that is makes the self-concept specific. If, in Ortega's words, "the mass is all that which sets no value on itself—good or ill—based on specific grounds," then the not-mass, the fully human individual, is he who *does* evaluate himself on specific grounds. He thinks of himself partly in terms of his particular competence and responsibilities. I certainly do not suggest that what a man can do is the same as what he is; far from it. But being a person is a process, and more a doing than a being, really; we are not statuary. Our error, in judging a man, lies not in attaching too much importance to what he can do, but in meaning by this: what can he do for *us?* what can we use him for?—rather than what he can do to further his own ends.

By helping the adolescent develop good, specific reasons for thinking well of himself, the school can contribute greatly to a stable identity. These reasons *are* competences, and adolescents with the help of good teachers can become very competent in mind, heart, and body. It is essential, however, that the adolescent think of this competence as his own and make it his own. The school must bring itself to recognize and respect a far wider variety of competence than it now does; more particularly, it must learn to accept the student's pride in his own distinction as well as to cultivate his participation in the things it thinks are important.

School ought to be a place where you can not only learn to *be* a scholar, a fighter, a lover, a repairman, a writer, or a scientist, but learn that you are *good* at it, and in which your awareness and pride in being good at it become a part of your sense of being you. More emphasis on the sciences, higher standards, stricter discipline: these, of themselves, will not help at all. They may hinder. A school that, while raising standards in certain academic areas, treats the student more than ever as an object or an instrument, simply becomes a more potent source of alienation.

What is needed is no program of technical training-cum-indoctrination, but the patient development of the kind of character and mind that conceives itself too clearly to consent to its own betrayal. It takes a kind of shabby arrogance to survive in our time, and a fairly romantic nature to want to. These are scarce resources, but more abundant among adolescents than elsewhere, at least to begin with. In the national interest they should be preserved. The greatest safeguard to any democracy is a continuing community of self-respecting young people who understand and accept their relationship to society. The basic unit of such a community is a stable self to respect.